This book has been produced under a private agreement with the author. All costs for research, preparation and production have been borne by private funding. No taxpayer funding was used. The contents do not reflect the views of either SCORE or any federal agency.

A SCORE® *That Counts*

The Story of the
Service Corps of Retired Executives

by

Elwyn A. Nellis

Illustrations by Daphne Stammer

Library of Congress Cataloging-in-Publication Data

Nellis, Elwyn A., 1910-
A SCORE that counts.

Includes bibliographic references.
1. SCORE (Organization) 2. Business consultants--United States. 3. Retired executives--United States. 4. Voluntarism--United States. I. Service Corps of Retired Executives Association. II. Title.
HD69.C6N45 1989 361.7'63'0973 89-10600
ISBN 0-9623466-0-8

First Edition

Printed in the United States of America by
Reproductions, Incorporated
12401 Washington Avenue
Rockville, Maryland 20852

Dedicated to.....

.....the unsung heroes of SCORE who, through the years and without any thought of personal gain or public recognition, have translated their skill and experience into a commodity that can be used by the swelling ranks of small business. Without them there would be no SCORE.

The Author

An Accolade

IF ever you feel that the ripples have gone unnoticed from the pebble you have dropped in the waters that wash the economic shores of the Nation -- pause a moment. The 2.5 million pebbles, pebbles just like yours, that have been dropped in the same waters over the last 25 years have created -- well, perhaps not a tidal wave, but a splash big enough, high enough, and shining enough to be seen and appreciated by the CEO of the world's largest business.

THE WHITE HOUSE

WASHINGTON

June 9, 1989

I am pleased to send warm greetings and congratulations to all those celebrating the 25th anniversary of the Service Corps of Retired Executives (SCORE).

Each of you can be proud of your participation in SCORE's efforts because they represent the finest American tradition of neighbor helping neighbor. During the past quarter-century, SCORE volunteers have generously shared their experience and expertise with more than 2.5 million small business people. This generosity has made a significant positive impact on small business in our country, revitalized depressed areas, encouraged individual enterprise, and spurred the creation of new jobs. The Service Corps of Retired Executives Association has done much to foster the American entrepreneurial spirit, and I applaud your fine work.

Barbara joins me in sending best wishes for this milestone anniversary and for continued success in the future.

Acknowledgments

This book would not have been possible without the help of many persons, both inside and outside the SCORE organization. The author is especially grateful to Priscilla W. McNeil, office administrator of the National SCORE Office, for her help in locating files and letters, for preparing the manuscript for typesetting, and for her advice and counsel; to Mark A. Sewell, editor of The SAVANT, for typesetting the text; to Margaret M. Hickey, Small Business Administration librarian, whose fine detective work located former SBA employees; and to George H. Kuechler, SCORE member from Sarasota, Florida, who provided important background material.

Contents

Illustrations

Foreword

Celebration.

We are a nation that loves celebration. As individuals, we celebrate family events. As a people, we celebrate local and national events. Organizations also find cause to celebrate milestones and events in their lifetimes.

SCORE recently celebrated three such events. In 1984 we observed the 20th anniversary of our founding. In 1987, based on records of national counseling activities over 23 years, Boston, Massachusetts, Chapter 20 counseled SCORE's two millionth client. And in 1988 the tenth anniversary of the National SCORE Office was observed.

Harry B. Matzen

The last two events became the prelude to SCORE's 25th anniversary and bolstered the early planning that started immediately after the 1987 National Workshop in San Diego. It was decided that the next bi-annual workshop would be held during the first week of October 1989 so that it would coincide with SCORE's 25th anniversary.

Three members of the Board began preliminary planning following the San Diego meeting and, with the Board's concurrence, selected Baltimore, Maryland, as the site for the event. A permanent 25th anniversary committee was named in September 1988 to arrange the program.

Among the plans that were developed was the production of a SCORE history to recognize the events of the last 25 years. Selected to write the history was Elwyn A. Nellis, who, as a 15-year SCORE member, has lived a good part of it. He is a 40-year newspaper veteran, retiring in 1975 as managing editor of the Yakima, Washington, *Herald-Republic*. He spent 30 months for SCORE in Washington, D. C., as public relations director. He is the creator of The SAVANT and served as its editor for four years.

We tell our clients in counseling that if a business can survive for the first five years, it should be on the road to success. SCORE has survived five times five years and has never faltered in accomplishing its twofold mission of counseling and workshops to assist small business to succeed.

This "story of SCORE" will tell you how that was accomplished.

Harry B. Matzen, President
SCORE Association (FY1989-90)

Introduction

In the 25 years since the SCORE program was first announced nationwide by the Small Business Administration in October 1964, thousands and thousands of examples of the value of our volunteer services to small business have been cited. Newspapers carry stories about local businesses that credit their success to SCORE counseling. National magazines carry articles explaining the SCORE program and profiling our members. The fact that more than two million people have received our help is a remarkable story in itself.

John H. Titley

Members of Congress have their praise of the SCORE program entered into the *Congressional Record*. State governors have issued proclamations honoring our program because of its benefits to the small business communities. The Small Business Administration has said frequently that SCORE is its most valuable management assistance resource and that it could not function without SCORE.

This book, however, is not another repetition of more success stories, but rather the story of how the SCORE organization evolved through the years, as told by those who shaped its course. It's the story of the men, women, and events that made a difference.

Since its beginning in 1964, the organization has had to adapt to the needs of the times. Sometimes these have resulted from changes in policies and priorities set by SBA. Sometimes they resulted from change in public law. In other instances new directions were in response to the growth in SCORE's membership and in the increasing demands of small business for SCORE's services.

With all the changes, however, the basic purpose of the organization -- to provide through experienced and qualified volunteers, free counseling and other technical and managerial guidance and training to existing and prospective businesses and nonprofit groups so they may increase their potential for success -- has never changed.

One of the most remarkable strengths of the organization is that there are still individuals actively involved in the policy-making process who were in at the beginning. This has provided that thread of continuity which has allowed SCORE membership to remain sharply focused on the basic purpose of helping small business. The SCORE organization has been fortunate in the choice of people it has selected to lead it through the years. Its presidents and directors have had the dedication and singleness of vision to see the goal and to hold fast to the purpose.

Looking back over the changes that have occurred in the first quarter century leads one to wonder what the next 25 years will bring. Based on the past record, one can only predict that while there will be changes, SCORE's focus will remain true.

Some of the changes are already occurring. One is the movement into electronic data processing to replace many of the clerical tasks. This already is well in place in the Washington national office with its extensive computer capability, including The SAVANT's desk-top publishing. [Editor's Note: The type for this book was set and formatted on The SAVANT's equipment.]

Every day more chapters are using their personal computers to facilitate their activities. It is conceivable that eventually all activity reports will be transmitted electronically and all chapters will be tied together at the district level by a computer network.

Another recent trend that may continue into the future is the rising interest by foreign governments asking for our help to put in place SCORE-like programs so their small businesses will be able to make stronger contributions to the foreign countries' economic growth. It is not beyond the realm of possibility that there might be a subsidiary SCORE group stationed overseas to help organize these programs.

Certainly, the demographic changes that are occurring will have a major impact in the year 2000 and beyond on the success of small businesses. The shrinking and aging of the work force in the face of growing technological advances will result in increased labor costs and stiff competition for qualified employees. These changes in the work force, when combined with an increasing global economy, will present a whole new range of challenges facing small businesses and our SCORE counselors.

What organizational changes will be required to enable our membership to meet these challenges is difficult to predict. It is clear from our history, however, that appropriate changes will be made and the challenges met. That has been the story of the SCORE organization through the years.

John H. Titley, Past President
SCORE Association (FY 1989-90)

Chapter 1

Any Place, USA

(There is no Hub Benson, nor is there a Sam Sebastian. But between them they illustrate SCORE's finest moments.)

When Sam Sebastian closed the door on Sam's Automotive Repair Shop he did it slowly, gently, almost as one would lower the lid on a coffin. The next time the door would be opened would be when his creditors came to remove the remains of a dream.

Sam was a good mechanic; one of the best. He could listen to a motor, much like a doctor listens to and reads a patient's vital signs, and diagnose the motor's ills. His fingers, though work thickened and heavy, were gentle and their touch as delicate as a surgeon's. And his knowledge of motors, large and small, was vast.

Sam was a good mechanic; there was no doubt of that. He was a good mechanic but a poor businessman. Three years ago he had quit his job in a garage, had withdrawn the $5,000 in his savings account -- the product of 25 years punching time clocks, scrimping and saving -- and had gone into business for himself. And now, at 43, he was defeated. Tomorrow he would make the rounds, looking for a job.

Failure is a bitter pill. Coated with shame, it is difficult to swallow. Once Sam would have laughed had anyone accused him of having pride. Pride in his work, perhaps, but *pride* -- that was something different. Self confidence had eroded, erased by shame; shame over having to face his friends and neighbors, his wife and his three sons. Especially his three sons. In them there had been deep pride, pride in their Old Man who had his own business.

Water welled up in Sam's eyes. He fought back the tears but one escaped. He wiped at it with a grease stained finger. It left a black smudge across his cheek.

It was not lack of customers that had licked Sam. There always had been plenty of customers -- so many, in fact, Sam had hired two mechanics to help him. He had just given the two young men their last pay checks and they had left in haste. They liked Sam. He was fair, a good teacher. But age and experience had not yet taught them how to handle the pain in Sam's eyes.

A part of Sam's hurt was that he did not understand what had happened. Business had been good but there always seemed to be more money going out than coming in. The $5,000 nest egg had disappeared like sand down a hole.

A deep sigh, more like a groan, rumbled from Sam's chest, and as he turned from the locked door a pickup stopped by the curb. It was not a work pickup but one of those that are popular as second cars. In its bed was a lawnmower. A spry, grey-haired man stepped down from the cab.

"Hi," the man said. "Glad I caught you before you got away. My lawnmower quit."

Sam was slow to respond and when he spoke there was a catch in his voice. "Sorry," he rasped, "we're closed."

The man's eyebrows shot up. "Closed! What do you mean? Closed! You're here, aren't you? All you have to do is unlock the door."

Sam shook his head. "You don't understand. We're closed. For good. Gone out of business."

The man's eyebrows climbed higher. "Say! I'm sorry about that! I hear you're the best damned mechanic around. What happened?"

Sam shrugged. "Couldn't make it pay. And now my creditors have slapped liens on all my equipment. You'll have to take your mower some other place."

The man's eyebrows slowly settled into their normal position. "Hmmm," he said. "Hmmm. I don't want to stick my nose in where I have no business but maybe I could help." He fished in his shirt pocket and took out a card case. He handed a card to Sam. "Name's Benson. Used to be in business myself. Now I'm retired. Play a little golf, play with the grandkids, mow the lawn when the mower works, but most of all I do a little business counseling." He pointed at the card in Sam's hand. "I work with SCORE. The Service Corps of Retired Executives."

Sam moved to return the card. "I can't afford any help. I'm busted!"

Benson shook his head. "Won't cost you a cent. We work for nothing."

A puzzled look crossed Sam's face. "Nobody works for nothing," he said.

"We do. All SCORE members are volunteers. We used to be in business and during that time we learned a little about making a business tick. Now we get our kicks from helping small businesses like yours to succeed. Simple."

Sam scowled. He was having difficulty trying to understand why someone who obviously lived on Carriage Hill would be willing to help some poor snook who had difficulty balancing a checkbook. It made him a little defiant.

"Hah!" he snorted. "You couldn't help me!"

Benson spread his hands. "We counseled about

150,000 small businesses last year," he said. "Some we helped. Some we didn't. I wouldn't know if I could help you unless I tried."

"What would you do?" Sam demanded.

"We-l-l," Benson replied, "the first thing I'd do would be to try to get those lien holders off your back. Give you a little breathing room. Then we'd work on your business practices." He paused. "It's a lot like fixing a motor, Sam. You can't fix it without first finding out what's wrong with it."

Benson's full name was Harry U. Benson. No one knew what the "U" stood for unless it was Benson himself and he wasn't saying. His friends called him "Hub." His enemies, of whom there were a few, called him other things. But never to his face. His two daughters called him "Dad." "Dad" is a pretty common name but it is not the word so much that counts, it's the way it's said that is the measure of a man. His wife called him -- but that's another story.

Except for college and time in the navy during World War II, Benson had spent his entire working life with a chain of department stores. He had started in the stock room evenings and weekends while in high school and was a zone manager of nine stores and a vice president of the chain when he retired.

Benson was not a workaholic but he had learned soon that he was ill prepared for retirement. Time weighed heavily on his hands. He had become uncharacteristically irritable. There were too many hours and too little to do. He had tried dropping in at his old store "just to see how things were going," but soon saw that while everyone was pleasant to him he no longer was a member of the team. He felt rebuffed. Logic told him this wasn't true, but logic and emotion have little in common. He had stayed home more, feeling sorry for himself. Relations with his wife of 30 years had become strained.

Then he joined SCORE. He saw in it an opportunity to put to use the skills and experience he had acquired through the years and to return to the community some of the benefits he had derived from it.

But there turned out to be more. He had always subscribed to the theory that "a job worth doing was worth doing well." When he saw the potential that was being wasted in his SCORE chapter because of a lack of goal oriented leadership, he had decided to run for chapter chairman.

He made it. And he remade the chapter. But not without some blood letting. The roster was leaner now, there were more training sessions, the case load was nearly doubled and workshops were on the agenda. And, not surprisingly, the morale of the chapter had improved.

Now they wanted him to accept an appointment as District Representative. He wasn't sure if he would accept; he liked the one-on-one contacts with the Sam Sebastians.

It's difficult to say what prompted Benson to impulsively offer his assistance to Sam. Perhaps it was the knowledge that it was people like Sebastian who through dreams, grit and determination sought to improve their lives while, in the process, they were improving the world in which they lived. Or perhaps it was something selfish. Benson had spent his life meeting and dealing with problems and perhaps he saw in the repair shop an opportunity to sink his teeth into still another problem and shake it into submission.

Whatever the reason, the Benson/Sebastian team swung into action. The following day they called upon Sam's local creditors and telephoned those in other cities. By the end of the day Benson had succeeded in getting all of them to agree to hold off on executing their liens.

In the cluttered, greasy, smelly cubbyhold Sam called his office the two grinned at each other.

"Jeez!" said Sam, "I'm sure glad you're not a salesman trying to sell me something!"

"Aw," Benson replied, "it wasn't that hard. We had something going for us."

"What was that?"

"Each of your creditors knows that if he exercises his lien, all he's going to get is nickels and dimes on what you owe. If he waits, he just might get everything you owe. And if what we're trying to do doesn't work, he still will get his nickels and dimes. It wasn't much of a gamble."

"Jeez!" Sam said again. "Are there many of you SCORE guys around?"

Benson laughed. It was a dry laugh. Without humor. "That depends on which set of figures you look at. Across the country there are about 12,000."

Sam whistled. "That many!"

"No. Only about half of them are active. Locally we have 39 members. All fairly active. But you have to remember that at our ages things can go wrong. It seems that all of the time there are at least one or two in the hospital for repairs. And there are some who, as soon as the birds start flying south, pack up their bags and go along."

"Yeah."

Benson wasn't sure if he had lost his audience or not but he was wound up. "There are 15 million small businesses in the country right now. That's about 10 million more than there were 20 years ago. Not all of them, of course, need our help but a fifth of them probably do. That's three million. Divide that by the number of active SCORE counselors and we're stretched pretty thin."

"I'm sure glad one of the thin pieces needed his lawnmower fixed. Now that we got those lien guys off my back, what do I do next?"

Benson sighed. "Not you, Sam. Us. I'll stick with you as long as you need me. Tomorrow we'll go over your books."

That was easy. It was easy because Sam didn't have any books. He carried his business around in his head. Trying to find out what should have been in the books, had there been any books, took three days. The closest thing to a calculator Sam had was a pencil with an eraser on it. His pricing system was a mixture of maybes, guesses and seat-of-the-pants estimates.

Even so, Benson found the business to be in better condition than he had anticipated. Sam's Automotive Repair Shop was a basket case but the basket at least had handles on it.

It was obvious to Benson that if Sam was going to continue in business he would need a loan. And Benson was not at all confident a bank would make a loan to a business with equipment covered by liens. They had two things going for them, though, Sam's skill and Benson's reputation.

A SCORE member is not supposed to build a business plan for a client; a client is supposed to do that with a SCORE member's help. In Sam's case, Benson made an exception. Time was of the essence; even Sam's wife was running out of sugar bowl money.

Visiting banks was not easy; Sam was embarrassed and Benson's confidence needed a morale boost, especially after two banks turned them down. The third bank, though, ran a rainbow across the sky. It agreed to grant a small loan, not as large as Benson had hoped but large enough to keep the wolf from nipping at Sam's heels.

Sam's Automotive Repair Shop was back in business. The two young mechanics were rehired and a part-time accountant/bookkeeper was added to the payroll. There were a lot of other things to do, of course, but in less than a month Benson had turned Sam's business from a failure into one that had a reasonable chance to succeed.

"I don't know how to pay you," Sam told Benson. "Is there anything I can do for you?"

Benson puckered his brow. "As a matter of fact, Sam, there is. Fix my lawnmower! I'm tired of paying that no-good kid next door $5 an hour to half mow my lawn."

Sam grinned. "It's already fixed," he said. "You forgot to put gas in the tank."

"May your fears and apprehensions be scratched in sand; may your achievements be etched in gold."

Walter H. Channing, President Emeritus, National SCORE Association, from a speech at a SCORE dinner in Washington, DC, September 9, 1988

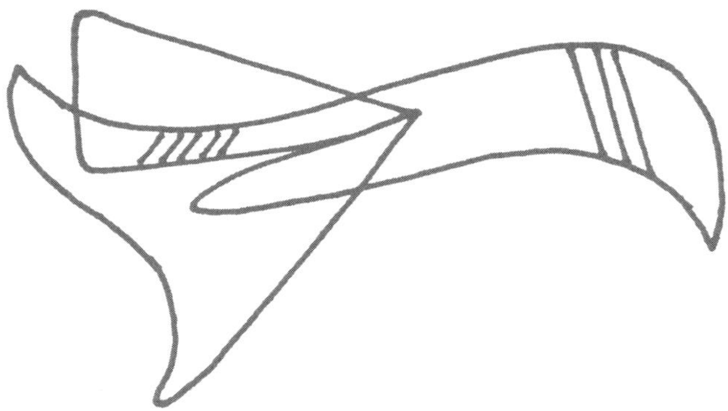

Chapter 2

Genesis I

Federally sponsored counseling for small business did not start with SCORE. Or with SBA. It probably started with RFC, SWPC, OSB/DOC, or SDPA. Or even perhaps in some other agency in the sea of alphabet soup that inundated Washington, D. C., just prior to and during World War II. Before that, while the federal government gave lip service to the importance of small business, most of the government's attention was focused on big business. If small business happened to benefit from this attention, that probably called for a homespun soliloquy out among the hustings. Back in those days politicians orated for votes, not for honoraria.

In any event, whatever federal small business counseling there was in those early days, it was almost as rare as feathers on a bowling ball. It was not until SCORE arrived on the scene that such counseling ballooned into a viable enterprise. In 25 years SCORE has counseled more than two million clients, and the surface has barely been scratched. Without SCORE, small business counseling would wither like the leaves in autumn. Countless jobs would disappear.

As the Great Depression was grinding the American economy into dust in the early Nineteen Thirties, President Hoover created the Reconstruction Finance Corporation (RFC); but before it had a chance to make much of an impact, there was a change of tenants in the White House and RFC was adopted by the Roosevelt Administration.

RFC's primary function was not to counsel business, large or small, but to provide business with money in the form of loans so business, in turn, could put people back to work. And since droves of people returning to work in big business had more visibility than two or three persons returning to work in small business, big business got the lion's share of RFC's attention.

It has to be presumed that RFC did some business counseling while doling out huge sums of money, but the counseling was not so much on "how" as it was on "what" and "where."

There is a story, perhaps apocryphal but nonetheless illustrative, of how RFC operated. Hotel space was tight to non-existent in Washington during World War II. Guests were limited to three-day stays. Sometimes less. One evening at dinner Jesse Jones, the Texas business tycoon who headed RFC, was seated next to the head of a large hotel chain.

After lamenting the shortage of hotel rooms, Jones "counseled" the innkeeper to build a new hotel in D. C.

"RFC will give you five million dollars to build it," he told the innkeeper. Before dessert a deal was struck and a new hotel began to take shape on some of Washington's choicest real estate "for the war effort."

Washington's appetite for alphabet soup seemed insatiable in those days; its solution to many problems was to create another bureaucracy. As the country entered World War II it soon became apparent many small businesses would go to the wall if they did not get a share of defense work. Congress created the Small War Plants Corporation (SWPC) to help small manufacturers procure initial defense contracts and subcontracts from large defense plants. Again, counseling, if there was any, was directed at just a small segment of the small business community -- manufacturers -- and was more or less limited to how and where the small plants could get a slice of government business. Little or no attention was directed towards how to successfully manage a business.

There's no doubt that SWPC rendered a valuable service to the country and to small manufacturers before its demise at the end of the war. But it also provided another lasting benefit -- the framework of SBA's procurement program came from SWPC.

When SWPC was abolished, its lending and property disposal powers were transferred to RFC while its other duties were transferred to the Office of

Small Business (OSB) in the Department of Commerce (DOC).

OSB was convinced that SWPC had not been sufficiently concerned with the day-to-day problems of small business. It contended, and rightly so, that many small business owners needed education and training in the basics of business.

RFC was a strong agency in those days and OSB was but a tiny sub-group in a weak DOC. It simply was not provided with sufficient funds to carry out its convictions and had to content itself with producing a few brochures and counseling only when an entrepreneur happened to wander into its office.

There matters stood until the Korean War when the Small Defense Plant Administration (SDPA) was formed to do pretty much what SWPC had done during World War II. SDPA, though, lacked one tool; lending powers were retained by RFC. The result was that SDPA barely got off the ground before it was abolished.

That left RFC as the main link between business and the federal government. RFC, in its heyday, performed great service to the country. It is credited with saving the country's banking system, with keeping many large corporations afloat, and with helping to finance World War II. But when the war was over, RFC sailed along, dispensing great gobs of money hither and yon on the theory such largess was necessary to convert the country from a war time to a peace time economy. Pent up buying power on the part of the people blew a hole in RFC's theory and Congress, fearful that too much money in the pipeline would overheat the economy, told RFC to lower its big guns and to put more emphasis on small business.

RFC apparently was not listening. It continued its spending ways while its attention to small business consisted of loans to such things as fish hatcheries, night clubs, snake farms, resort hotels and movie houses.

The handwriting was on the wall. Congressional hearings were held and RFC started to disappear into history.

Almost as an afterthought, Congress remembered the small business votes out in the boondocks. On May 14, 1953, as RFC lay dying, the House Committee on Banking and Currency began hearings on a bill to establish the Small Business Administration. Six days later the comparable committee in the Senate began its hearings on its version of a Small Business Administration bill. By the end of July all differences had been resolved between the two bills, and Congress passed the Small Business Act on July 29, 1953. The following day President Eisenhower signed the bill into law.

SBA was born.

When RFC was at its peak it had more than 15,000 employees. When SBA was started it had fewer than 500, most of whom were alumni of RFC. This perhaps helps to explain why SBA's emphasis has been upon loans even though the law establishing it said the federal government "should aid, counsel, assist and protect the interests of small business."

Counseling small business in management practices was written into the law.

But there was a problem. Even as SBA grew into regions, districts, and branch offices across the country, there never were enough management assistance officers -- fewer than 100 to serve an estimated five million small businesses. Meanwhile, a strange thing was happening to the economy; new small businesses were springing up all over. The MAOs became the most harried, hurried and harassed of all the employees in the federal government.

To their credit, though, they managed to counsel 14,000 clients in 1963 and 34,000 the following year. Some even managed to circuit ride out into the hinterlands to help struggling entrepreneurs in the backwaters of the nation. The load, though, was heavy; the MAOs averaged less than an hour per client which meant that most of their "counseling" was limited to handing out SBA publications. In 1965, more than four million were distributed. Free. Even if they had been equipped with seven-league boots -- something Congress neglected to provide -- the MAOs could not possibly do the job Congress had laid upon them.

Obviously, something had to be done. And something was done. But to reach that point the pages of history have to be turned back a dozen years, back to Wilmington, Delaware, and to a man by the name of Maurice du Pont Lee. Lee was at loose ends. After a long and outstanding career as an engineer at E. I. du Pont de Nemours and Company, he became a victim of company policy -- he was put out to pasture at age 65.

Lee accepted the inevitable but he wasn't happy about it. He was not about to let himself be relegated to what he called "the brain graveyard." Fortunately, there were others in Wilmington who felt the same way. He gathered together a small group of retirees, all far from brain dead, and they formed the Consulting and Advisory Services, Inc.

Although all members of the group had come from large corporations, they realized that the backbone of any economy rests upon the shoulders of the small business person. They also realized that many small business persons were ill equipped to reach the highest potential of their efforts. It was upon this latter group that the Consulting and Advisory Services was focused. The goal of the group was to make Wilmington a better place in which to live.

One of Lee's first cases came to him not so much as a member of the consulting group but as a businessman. He was approached by a real estate agent who was trying to sell a piece of commercial property that was on the sick side. The owner was a widow in dire need of funds. Lee learned that the property was mortgaged and was being managed by a management firm set up for the sole purpose of handling the property. He dug a little deeper and learned that the property's illness could be corrected with better management. There was a smell of fraud in the air, an odor that was confirmed when Lee was offered a bribe of $10,000 to disappear into the sunset.

Working with the real estate agent, Lee fumigated the atmosphere, put the property on a paying basis and, when the property was sold, got substantially more for it than was being asked originally. Lee was happy. The agent was happy. The widow was happy. The management firm was not so well pleased.

While SBA's MAOs were struggling to meet the demands for their services, Lee's group in Wilmington was chalking up an enviable record of success. What's more, the concept was spreading. By 1963 there were nearly 50 similar organizations across the land. Some of the groups charged nominal fees for their services, but for most groups, their services were free. Some of the groups lasted but a short time; others demonstrated better staying power.

One such group was located in Boston and a member, a man by the name of Harvey C. Krentzman, suggested to SBA that the concept be adopted by SBA. SBA rejected the proposal. It said it did not have sufficient management assistance personnel to start a new program.

There is an old saying that nothing can stop an idea whose time has come, and it must be true. SBA soon saw the wisdom of Krentzman's suggestion, saw a chance to add thousands of experienced business persons to its staff at virtually no cost, and gathered the concept to its bosom. On October 5, 1964, SBA Administrator Eugene P. Foley, during ceremonies in Boston, officially launched SCORE. Other kick-off sessions were held in other cities and by the end of the month SCORE had 2,000 members

To the MAOs, SCORE's arrival must have seemed like the arrival of the cavalry in a Grade B movie. As things turned out, though, it wasn't a classic, textbook cavalry charge; the troops encountered a few gopher holes along the way.

"Not what we give, but what we share --
For the gift without the giver is bare."

James Russell Lowell

Chapter 3

Genesis II

Unlike Minerva, who in Roman mythology sprang full grown from the head of Jupiter, SCORE has had to do it the old-fashioned way -- by the long and sometimes chaotic process of evolution. There is, though, a relationship. Minerva, among other things, was the goddess of wisdom and skill, attributes which SCORE has in abundance. In her legacy to SCORE, however, Minerva failed to insert a tiny slip of paper much like those found in modern Christmas toys: "Some assembling may be necessary."

Dr. Grant C. Moon, a former member of the SBA central office staff, in his doctoral dissertation on SCORE's beginning years, observed that SCORE's evolution has "vacillated between crisis and tranquility." He attributed this in large part to SBA's lack of planning. He pointed out that SBA did not consider organization realignment, legal commitments, use of

SCORE for personal gain, infringement in the professional counseling field, and the amount of time SBA would need to administer the program.

In all fairness, SBA did investigate possible infringement in the professional counseling field; and while there were some professionals who protested, a few vociferously, the general feeling was that SCORE would be working in a field that could ill afford the services of professionals.

SCORE, as originally conceived, was no more than a list of names of available counselors. When SCORE was created SBA launched a media campaign to introduce the new service. Some of the stories were so glowing and so well written one could almost see the flags wave and hear the drums roll. In one of the initial stories, under the by-line of Eugene P. Foley, SBA Administrator, Foley said, "We have devised a simple form in which retired executives can describe their experience or interest in counseling and indicate their wish to organize or join such a group. Completed forms will be carefully classified and analyzed. An inventory will be published at some central point, along with a roster of potential leaders."

That was the original SCORE organization. Simple. Nothing fancy. Just a list of names.

Even here, though, there was a glitch. In none of the stories was it mentioned that counselors would donate their services. In the first month following the kick-off in Boston, 2,000 potential volunteers flocked to the banner. And by the end of the year, after they had learned there would be no income from their efforts, half the original had dropped out.

Perhaps the biggest stumbling block in SCORE's formation was SBA's failure to assess the time that would be required to administer the program. The publicity that drew the volunteers into SCORE also brought in a flood of clients. The poor MAOs, previously laboring under the load of trying to counsel a substantial portion of the five million small businesses, suddenly were confronted with mountains of paper work generated by the counselors. The rapid acceleration of SCORE made it difficult, if not impossible, for SBA to keep abreast with the administration of the new program. Assisting small businesses in the management of their affairs is but one function of SBA, but the shower of SCORE-generated paper work placed such a burden upon SBA's small staff, other functions of the agency had to be neglected.

This was an intolerable situation. Here was a program that was not supposed to cost anything but that was, in fact, costing SBA a bundle. According to Dr. Moon, the SCORE program in the first six months of 1966 cost SBA $700,000 in staff time. That amounted to $60 a case. It can be argued, of course, that the work done by those early day volunteers, had it been done by SBA employees, would have cost SBA a couple of million dollars, thereby saving SBA more than a million dollars. The trouble with that argument is that SBA didn't have the extra $700,000 to invest.

After all the fanfare and publicity launching the program, SBA could hardly come out and say, "Oops, we goofed. This program is going to take a few million dollars a year just to run."

No. It couldn't do that. There had to be another way. And there was. It was the volunteers themselves who provided the answer. As SBA looked out over its cadres of volunteers, SBA saw that there was a vast amount of man-hours going to waste in-between counseling cases. If those man-hours could be converted into membership rosters, skills rosters, assignment rosters and case reports, the problems would be solved. That, of course, would require some sort of a formal organization, which was no problem -- organize the groups into chapters and let them elect officers and all that.

The volunteers did not object to formalizing their relationships. It gave them a sense of belonging and provided them with an opportunity to sit around and swap yarns with their peers, a sort of service club/social club atmosphere. One chapter even converted its organization into a quasi pinochle club.

Formation of chapters was accepted readily enough by the volunteers; paper work was quite another thing. It was not well received and therein began the litany still recited today: "I didn't join

SCORE to do paper work; I joined to counsel small business."

But the idea worked. After a fashion. Paper work at the MAO level actually did drop off, not 100 per cent but enough to bring the cost factor down to a manageable level.

While chapter formation proceeded smoothly enough, the sequential numbering system did not. Since the program was kicked off officially in Boston, that city could make a valid claim for the No. 1 slot. But no. Because SBA had run a pilot SCORE project in Washington, D. C., before the Boston celebration, the chapter in the nation's capital became No. 1.

Then how about No. 2 for Boston? Nope. That went to Minneapolis, hometown of Administrator Foley. Boston wound up as No. 20 and Wilmington, where the whole idea originated more than a decade before, was designated as No. 42. A part of the problem was that there was no official listing of chapters until early 1965 when all chapters were lumped together and given the same starting dates. The real numerical sequence was lost in the shuffle.

Chapters, once formed, had to have some sort of official paper to be recognized as chapters. "Charter" had a good ring to it and Richard M. Sweeney, an SBA employee who also was involved in the Boy Scouts of America, wrote the master charter, using the Boy Scout troop charter as his guide. It is still in use today.

Minerva, being a goddess, knew all about Fate. SBA and SCORE, being made up of mere mortals, were not so well informed and were totally unprepared when Fate, in the guise of a *Reader's Digest* article in 1967, appeared on the scene. Previously there had been many stories written about SBA's volunteer counseling program but none had the impact of the *Reader's Digest* contribution. Written by Harmon Tupper, it first appeared in *Harvest Years*. When the condensed version appeared in *Reader's Digest* SCORE took off like a runner hyped up on steroids. New chapters sprang up like mushrooms after a spring rain and SBA had a new problem -- how to keep track of and manage the suddenly expanded program. What SBA needed was some sort of a one-stop shopping center, a national organization to bring all the chapters together in a network.

A man by the name of Sam Goldman in Miami, Florida, was among the first to see the advantages of a national organization. In 1967 he polled all the SCORE chapters to plumb their interest in forming such a group. The response was not overwhelming.

Later in the year, though, SBA called selected SCORE volunteers from around the country to a meeting in Silver Spring, Maryland, to discuss the formation of a national organization. Speeches were made, papers read and suggestions advanced. One of the proposals was to hire "dollar-a-year" circuit riders to work with the chapters.

The balloon must have been made of lead. It sank.

The following year SBA called a second meeting. This time SBA Administrator Howard J. Samuels had a new idea. He wanted SCORE to change directions and concentrate on helping minority businesses in targeted areas.

SCORE didn't like that. The delegates could see no difference between counseling small minority businesses and counseling small businesses. Come one. Come all.

Came 1969. A new meeting. A new administrator -- Hilary Sandoval, Jr. Same old proposal. Concentrate on minorities.

The delegates didn't like Sandoval's proposal any better than they had liked Samuels' the year before. A national organization was as far away as it was when Miami's Goldman first proposed it.

Perseverance is a wonderful thing. It usually pays off. SBA called still another meeting in 1970 and this time there was progress. A committee, called the National Planning Committee, was formed for the express purpose of planning still another meeting -- this one to be a national SCORE conference made up of representatives from all qualified chapters in the country.

The 154 delegates gathered in Atlanta late in October 1970, and through a day and a half they discussed the need for and the advantages of bringing all SCORE chapters under the umbrella of a national organization. When it came time to vote the tally was

154 "for" and 0 "against." The planning committee became the National SCORE Committee and was designated as the "voice of SCORE." What the committee was to vocalize on was not spelled out in any detail, but SCORE did have an embryonic organization, one that was established not by a few farsighted SCORE members but by 154 SCORE delegates representing their peers back home.

It was a heady moment, filled with euphoria. But euphoria, as everyone knows, is a transient thing. Within a matter of months SBA, without consulting the fledgling organization, transferred SCORE from management assistance to SBA's loan department to service small business delinquent loans.

Bill collectors!

There is a vast difference between counseling small business and collecting money from deadbeats or trying to extract blood from a stone. SCORE, individually and by chapters, sent SBA a message. SCORE membership dropped, recruiting fell off, and some clients went without counseling.

The new organization was confronting its first crisis. Though weak as an organization, the struggle to create the National SCORE Committee had produced some strong leaders who had better than 20/20 vision. One such leader was Walter H. Channing of Royal Oak, Michigan.

Channing is an unusual man. He is small in stature and mild of voice, hardly a picture of a dynamic leader. Yet his counsel and guidance have helped SCORE emerge into the organization it is today. He has the rare ability to listen through many arguments, some logical and some emotional, and come up with a consensus that cuts through the fog and produces agreement. His calm analytical approach has taken him to the Hill so many times to testify before Congressional committees that he knows his way around the Halls of Congress better than some Congressmen.

Channing is both a provincial and a cosmopolitan man. He has spent his entire life in the Detroit area but has traveled so much he knows Paris or Antwerp or Fairbanks or Atlanta almost as well as he knows his native Detroit. His 25 years in SCORE constitutes a third career, his fourth if his service in the military is counted.

Channing's first career was in hands-on retailing and after 34 years with the same company he took retirement. In that 34 years, however, he spent four years on active military duty and 16 years in the reserves. As a matter of fact, he was lecturing on economics at a war college shortly after his retirement from business when he was tapped by the State Department to go to Europe as senior consultant in marketing and retail distribution for the Organization for European Economic Cooperation and Economic Development. That began his second career. Or was it his third? No matter. Between 1956 and 1982, because of his skill in retail merchandising, he made many trips to Europe to present ideas in business activity. He traveled behind the Iron Curtain. In Greece, because of his work there, he was named honorary president for life of the New Serres Chamber of Commerce and Industry.

He had just returned to Detroit from his first trip to Europe in 1964 when he saw in the newspaper one of the early stories about SCORE. The challenge intrigued him. He investigated and then became a charter member of what was to become the Detroit chapter. He served for a time as chapter chairman and was selected by SBA to attend the first meetings where the formation of a national organization was discussed.

When the plan for a national organization began to jell he became chairman of the National Planning Committee; and then, as the jell solidified, he became chairman of the National Committee.

The new organization, of course, proved to be inadequate and was tightened into a more formal organization which became the National SCORE Council. Channing was elected its first Chairman and subsequently served several terms as Vice Chairman.

In 1975 SCORE was incorporated into a nonprofit association and for the next seven or eight years there were two SCORE organizations -- the Council to handle the management of the SCORE program and the Association to handle the business of the nonprofit corporation. Boards of Directors of both bodies were the same. The Council was dissolved in 1982 and the

Walter H. Channing

Association now is the governing body of the entire organization. Channing has served as President Emeritus of both bodies.

While serving on the national level, Channing did not neglect the home front. He served as District Representative for the State of Michigan and following the 1967 riots in Detroit he provided yeoman service to his community in getting the city back on its feet. Detroit was declared a disaster area and since most of the losses were in small retail establishments, Channing was selected by SBA to serve on the agency's disaster team.

Two things stood him in good stead -- his knowledge of retailing and the fact that he knew personally some of the stricken merchants. He established a formula under which fair estimates could be made to cover the losses, and Detroit emerged from the riots not unscathed but a lot more speedily than it would have, had it not been for Channing's help.

From his view through a quarter of a century of SCORE, Channing sees many changes down the road.

"The status quo no longer applies," he said recently. "In the future SCORE will need a growing number of new types of members versed in the developments that are taking place. Members will no longer be able to base advice on what took place years ago. Living standards are changing, there are problems of language, and what is now a minority market probably will become a majority market. SCORE must plan for the changes that are taking place."

There is another member of SCORE who also has an enviable record. He is Joseph G. E. Knight of West Warwick, Rhode Island. Knight also was present at those early formative meetings of the SCORE organization. Unlike Channing, though, who is quiet and calm, Knight is brusque and sometimes volatile. He has no reluctance to speak his mind, to ruffle feathers and to rub fur the wrong way. He served as Providence, Rhode Island, chapter vice chairman and chairman, was elected Regional Representative in Region I and then became President of the National SCORE Council. Following his terms on the Board of Directors of the National Council he returned to Rhode Island to again work in the SCORE trenches. Recently he emerged again on the national level as chairman of SCORE's newly formed National Advisory Council. On June 7, 1989, he was honored at a District SCORE meeting when the Providence chapter changed its name to the "Joseph G.E. Knight Chapter."

Knight, a native of England, in his early years had some difficulty trying to find himself. He was apprenticed to a furniture firm to learn retailing. Previously, he had spent some time in Italy and had learned to speak Italian. When the firm for which he was working learned he was bilingual he was sent to Italy. What the firm did not know was that while he could speak Italian he couldn't write it, a prerequisite for his job in Italy. That ended a budding relationship.

Back in England he entered the insurance business but wasn't too enthusiastic about the work; and when England was wracked by a general strike in 1926 he became a volunteer policeman, since the regular police were among the strikers. He found the work interesting although somewhat dangerous, and when his stint was over he decided to seek his fortune in the New World.

It was his intent to stay with relatives when he arrived in America, to give himself a chance to get his feet on the ground; but when he landed in Boston he discovered his relatives had moved to the Midwest. That presented a problem. He had to find a job. Immediately. And he did. As an automobile mechanic. The fact he didn't know much about automobiles did not deter him -- necessity is the mother of ingenuity. That job was followed by one as a shipper in a candy factory. He liked that job but only because he likes candy. He instinctively knew, though, that one cannot eat his way to success on a sweet tooth. So he left the gumdrops, the chocolates and the jawbreakers to become a bellhop. Again, that wasn't exactly what he was looking for as a career so he became a sheet metal worker in a furnace factory. Several injuries later he was on the lookout for other work, something that did not endanger his fingers and toes.

An advertisement in a Boston paper caught his attention. Sears, Roebuck & Company wanted some two-week temporary help. He applied, was hired, and

Joseph G. E. Knight

stayed on for 36 years, working in every phase of retail selling. He retired in 1964 at the age of 56 and immediately answered another newspaper ad, this one by SBA seeking SCORE volunteers.

Although active at the national level of SCORE, Knight has not neglected his roots. He conducts two workshops a month, counsels an average of six clients a week, and lectures at two community colleges (12 years) and at the Continuing Education Division of the University of Rhode Island (18 years).

Knight feels that one of SCORE's problems is a lack of standardization in its operations.

"We should have regional training centers so all leaders are equally versed in the operation," he said. "This would need funding, of course, and I don't think we can get it from SBA. Perhaps we might get the necessary funds from foundations. It would be worth a try."

There were other dedicated SCORE members who struggled in those early formative years, but Knight and Channing are the only two who have stayed at or close to the national level. Two of those early planners now are dead and two others are inactive or close to it. But in 1971 and beyond, it took the combined talents of all of them to keep SCORE from sinking into oblivion.

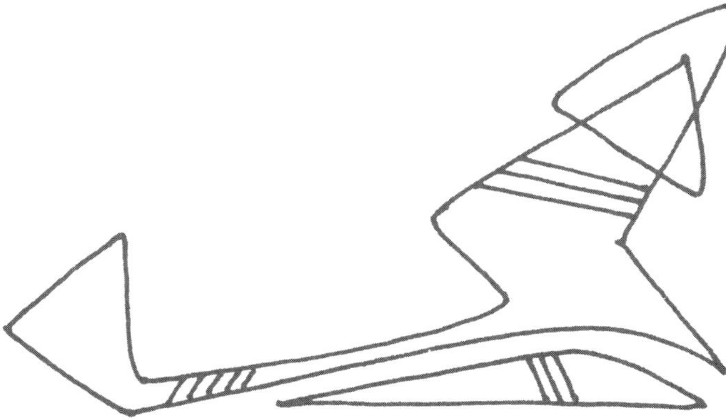

"Knowledge comes, but wisdom lingers."

Alfred, Lord Tennyson

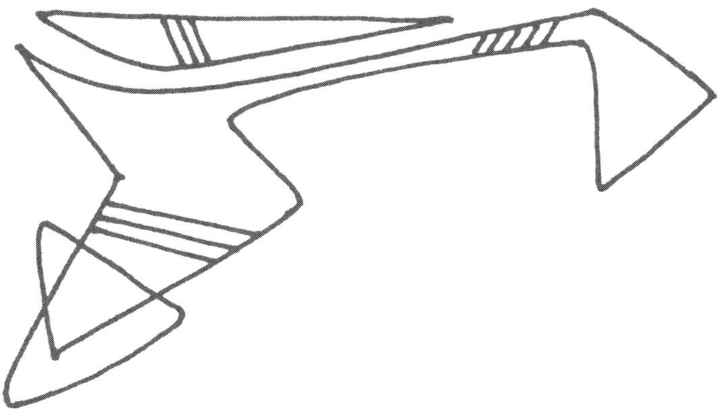

Chapter 4

The Call to ACTION

On a cold January day in 1961 John F. Kennedy made an inspiring plea to the American people. "Ask not what your country can do for you;" he said, "ask what you can do for your country." His words lit a torch of social consciousness that continues to burn today as brightly as the Eternal Flame at his gravesite in Arlington Cemetery. Born were such programs as the Peace Corps, Foster Grandparents, Volunteers in Service to America (VISTA) and others.

It was during those heady days of active altruism that SCORE was born, but it is doubtful if social consciousness played a significant role. To be sure, the SCORE program has social implications. Through its help to small business, employment is reduced, poverty diminished and standards of living raised, but SCORE's thrust is economic, not sociological.

Washington, D. C., is a political town. Federal government bends and sways in the various political winds that blow along the city's marble canyons. Agencies, particularly in the upper echelons of political appointees, try to catch the wind's direction and trim their sails accordingly. In the underbelly of career bureaucrats, where life is less frenetic, the buffeting winds are less apparent. Leaders come and go, but bureaucracy goes on forever.

Social action was the vogue when SCORE was born, but SCORE remained untouched by it until 1968. And again in 1969. Two SBA administrators, at meetings in Silver Spring, Maryland, told SCORE it should change directions and focus its attention on minority enterprises in target areas selected by SBA.

SCORE resisted the narrowed field of endeavor. It pointed out that its mandate was to serve all small business, minority or otherwise. SBA did not force the issue and there the matter stood. But not for long.

At one end of Pennsylvania Avenue President Richard M. Nixon cooked up a plan to bring all of the government's scattered social programs under one agency. He called the new agency ACTION, an acronym for the American Committee To Improve Our Neighborhood. To SCORE's surprise, it was caught in the broad sweep of the broom even though there was little similarity between it and the other programs. President Nixon's proposal was sent to the other end of Pennsylvania Avenue where Congress provided legislation to formalize the plan.

Lincoln A. Simon of Williamsburg, Virginia, now a member of SCORE, was SBA's director of the Office of Management Counseling Services at the time. He recalls that neither SBA nor SCORE had much advance warning that SCORE was about to be taken over by another agency. Even so, one thing is evident: SBA already had the mindset to transform SCORE from an economic endeavor into a more popular social program. Two administrators had tried to get the job done, only to be rebuffed by SCORE.

Even if the plan to sweep all socially oriented volunteers under one umbrella had been a good one, including SCORE was like a proverbial mixture of apples and pears. SCORE was economic, the others social. SCORE volunteers were unpaid, the other volunteers received stipends. And to make the apple/pear mutation even more grotesque, a part of SCORE was to remain under SBA while the remainder was to become a part of ACTION. SBA would be responsible for program operation, direction and oversight, while ACTION would be responsible for recruitment, publicity, chapter formation, new opportunities for volunteer services, and financing. In other words, SBA was to continue to get SCORE's services while another agency administered the program and picked up the tab.

SBA should have known better. It is aware of the Golden Rule as practiced in Washington: "He who has the gold makes the rules."

Simon puts it this way. "ACTION had financial responsibility for SCORE. That had considerable bearing upon the SCORE operation which was supposed to have been an SBA function."

Before the plan creating ACTION became a law, SCORE had an opportunity to testify on March 1, 1971, before the Government Operations Subcommittee of the House of Representatives. It was one of Walter Channing's first trips to the Hill for SCORE. His arguments were that SCORE was different from the other programs under the umbrella -- economic versus sociological; that it would be difficult, if not impossible, to work under two masters; and that the partial transfer would change the character of SCORE.

SCORE's arguments fell on deaf ears even though there was a minority report that backed SCORE in strong language. The outcome, though, was a foregone conclusion. It is revealed in an exchange between Rep. Samuel B. Rosenthal (NY), committee chairman, and Channing.

> Mr. Rosenthal: You understand that under the rules of the House there can be no amendments or changes in reorganization plans as compared to legislation. So if someone wanted to agree with the position you have taken he would have to vote against the reorganization plan or for the resolution of disapproval.
>
> Mr. Channing: We understand that, Mr. Chairman.
>
> Mr. Rosenthal: Is that the position you are urging upon the House?

Mr. Channing: That is the position, sir.

Neither the committee nor the House was about to throw out the reorganization plan simply because a small group of retired business executives objected to being placed under ACTION.

What SCORE predicted came to pass. SCORE funds for SBA work evaporated, counselors' claims for mileage went unpaid, and many of America's small businesses were left to dangle in the wind. With his hand on the purse, Michael Balzano, ACTION director, tried to funnel SCORE's resources into the inner cities to, among other things, give economic advice to the operators of soup kitchens.

These were trying and frustrating times for SCORE. And probably for SBA, too. Its counseling arm was in shambles. SCORE asked SBA to help get SCORE out from the sociological umbrella, but there is an unwritten rule in Washington that says an administration's agencies will not fight among themselves, and SBA was not about to break that rule. There were some informal meetings between SBA and ACTION officials, according to Simon, but ACTION resisted the transfer of SCORE back to SBA.

"No agency wants to lose a part of its functions," Simon said.

In addition to Channing there were three other players who had prominent roles in the ACTION drama. They were Lee R. Maxwell, Orville A. Rummel and Jay C. Lansford. All, at one time, were chairman of the national SCORE organization during its schizophrenic period.

Except for a few personal letters, little is known about Maxwell other than that he was from Florida and was Regional Representative in Region IV. The National SCORE Office, which now houses SCORE's archives, was not in existence during Maxwell's tenure on the committee and he had disappeared from the national scene before any records were collected. The few personal letters that are available, however, indicate that Maxwell, now deceased, was swimming against the current; he favored SCORE's continued affiliation with ACTION.

There is an up side to that, however. His activities on behalf of ACTION had a therapeutic effect -- they helped to illustrate to SCORE, to SBA, to Congress and to some people in the federal administration that the arrangement was a two-headed monster. There is evidence of this, more faint than concrete but still evidence. In 1972 SBA changed directions again and returned SCORE to management assistance from the loan division, a move that blew more life into what was rapidly becoming a moribund SCORE.

Orville A. Rummel of Woodburn, Oregon, was chairman of the 1974 SCORE conference in Denver, Colorado, a conference attended by ACTION and SBA salaried personnel as well as by SCORE delegates. In the closing moments of the session someone made a

Orville A. Rummel

motion to determine if SCORE wanted to remain under ACTION or to return wholly to SBA.

The motion took Rummel by surprise. Near pandemonium broke out. Rummel recalled later that "it sounded as though there were a thousand people in the room," all voting to remain under ACTION. The "nay" votes were drowned out by the "yeas."

Before Rummel could recover, a motion was made to adjourn the meeting; and since a motion to adjourn takes precedence over any other matters, the meeting ended amid cheers and howls of protest.

Rummel, as his name implies, is of German extraction, and rumor has it that Germans are a stubborn people. Whether true or not, Rummel is stubborn. When he gets his teeth into something, he hangs on. His background illustrates that.

A native of Chicago, Rummel went to work for Western Electric Company when he was 16. He enlisted in the army during World War I, went overseas, spent some time in a hospital as a result of a poison gas attack and then went to work for AT&T, of which Western Electric was a subsidiary. From time to time, AT&T transferred him around the country and he wound up in Seattle where he retired after 45 years with the company. During his Seattle years, though, he took time out to rejoin the army for World War II and was sent to Alaska. Following the war the army tried to send him to Japan, but his stubborn streak popped up. He had had enough of "soldiering" to suit him, so he resigned his commission and went back to work for AT&T. He joined SCORE in 1965 in Seattle and when he moved to Oregon he transferred to the Portland chapter. He became secretary, then chairman and then was elected Alternate Regional Representative for Region X. When George Shields, the Regional Representative, had to step down for health reasons, Rummel moved up to the RR slot. While chairman of the Portland chapter he became disillusioned with ACTION.

"It was tight with the buck," he explains. "ACTION made it difficult for SCORE to carry out its mission."

When the vote in Denver went so overwhelmingly against SCORE's return to SBA, Rummel set out to find out what had happened. What he discovered was not pretty. He learned that when the vote was taken a number of SCORE delegates already had left the meeting to catch planes to return home, and that ACTION salaried personnel, who had no vote, were the ones whose lung power had carried the day.

He was not about to let that stand. He and Jay Lansford, the national organization's treasurer from Dallas, Texas, polled all SCORE chapters by mail for their views about returning to SBA. The result was a foregone conclusion -- something like 88 per cent for getting out of ACTION.

Armed with the results of the referendum Rummel took a trip to Washington. He went up to the 10th floor at 1441 L Street, N. W., and walked in on SBA Administrator Thomas S. Kleppe.

"Tom," he said, "either you help SCORE get out of ACTION or I'll withhold all SCORE counseling for 60 days!"

It was a bluff and Kleppe probably suspected it was a bluff. But he couldn't be sure. After all, Rummel and Lansford had pulled off the referendum. Bluff or not, talks between SBA and ACTION heated up.

Rummel is no longer active in SCORE; he has become a Gold Card member.

"SCORE has grown enormously in my time," he said in a recent interview. "It has become a big business; paper work has piled up. I think each Region, and perhaps Districts, should have paid administrators to handle the business of SCORE. Their salaries should be paid by SBA but they should work only for SCORE."

His confrontation with Kleppe, of course, was not the only factor involved in SCORE's eventual return to SBA. Many letters were written to influential congressmen and to sympathetic members of the Ford Administration. Congressional hearings were attended.

And there was Jay Lansford. Lansford says he never really wanted to become chairman of the na-

Jay C. Lansford

tional organization but he got there anyway, succeeding Rummel. He had become too prominent in SCORE's fight to get out from under ACTION. During the annual SCORE conference in Florida the year before the Denver fiasco, he earned ACTION's enmity when he single-handedly put down an attempt by ACTION to give SCORE membership to all union leaders in the country.

In Denver he did not improve his reputation with ACTION. After listening to ACTION speakers tell SCORE it was going to have to become more involved in social programs and that if SCORE wanted funds for SCORE work, SCORE would have to go to Congress to get it, Lansford decided a response was in order.

If sufficiently riled, Lansford can become abrasive. He was sufficiently riled in Denver. He delivered a scorching speech in which he likened ACTION to the "ladies' auxiliary."

When the Denver vote went against SCORE, SCORE members gathered around Lansford.

"What'll we do?" they demanded.

"Nothing," he told them. "Not now. We've been outmaneuvered. Go home. And wait. The battle's not over yet."

Lansford is well suited for a fight. He is a tall Texan, built like a wedge and looks as though in his prime he might have been able to wrestle a Texas longhorn to the ground. He is a loquacious person, something that probably comes naturally. He spent years as a salesman, and when he retired from the Johnson Wax Company he was sales manager. That was in 1968. He spent some time playing golf but when he had had golf "up to the eyebrows" he decided to do some consulting. That turned out to be too much work so he joined SCORE. After two or three stints as Dallas chapter chairman he was elected Regional Representative in Region VI.

Alone, the efforts of Rummel and Lansford may have succeeded in divorcing SCORE from ACTION but there were other elements involved. ACTION had an advisory board and Walter Channing was a member as SCORE's representative. ACTION decided to make a production of presenting its annual report to President Gerald R. Ford and gave the report to the advisory board to hand carry to the White House. During the formalities President Ford went down the line, shaking the hands of all of the advisory board members. When he reached Channing, he paused.

"Hmmm," the President said. "From Michigan, I see."

He and Channing chatted for a few moments and discovered they had mutual interests and acquaintances. Then the President moved on down the line.

It was not long after, in July 1975, that President Ford signed an executive order returning SCORE to SBA's sole sponsorship. Channing denies any knowledge of any special ears that may have been bent, but there's always a question: How did an organization as small and as relatively insignificant as SCORE really become the object of a Presidential order?

Of course, there may be a simple explanation. SBA and ACTION may have become so tired of having a bunch of hornets buzzing around their heads that they went to the Office of Management and Budget and said, "Get those characters off our backs."

Even with the executive order, SCORE was not out of the woods. SCORE had been put under the joint supervision of SBA and ACTION by an Act of Congress. It was going to take another Act of Congress to undo the damage.

The wheels for that step already were moving when Lansford appeared before a congressional oversight committee to testify in favor of the transfer legislation. He made an impassioned plea but the wheels of Congress move slowly -- it was not until 1978 that Congress finally got around to passing the necessary legislation. Not all the delay, though, rested with Congress. An initial requirement was the preparation of the necessary legislation by SBA, something that did not seem to be very high on SBA's list of priorities.

Two other SCORE members -- Julius Davidson and Walter P. O'Rourke -- both of whom had played supporting roles in the ACTION drama, took the lead in pressuring SBA to take the final step.

"Every step of progress the world has made has been from scaffold to scaffold and from stake to stake."

Wendell Phillips, 1851

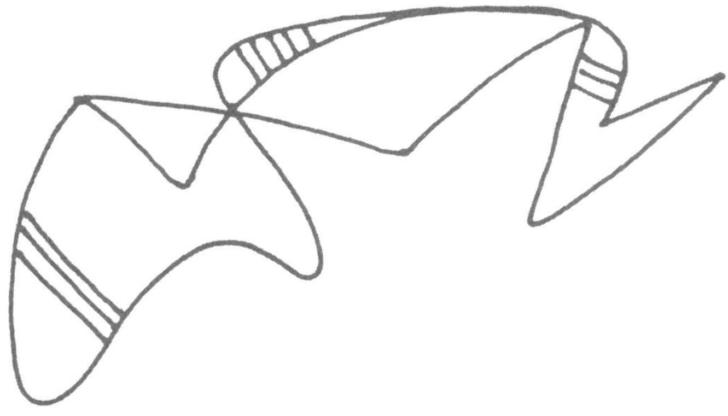

Chapter 5

The Middle Years

Julius Davidson and Walter P. O'Rourke, both now deceased, had something of a Damon and Pythias relationship. Both occupied desks in the National SCORE Office from the day it opened in 1978 -- Davidson as SCORE's budget director and O'Rourke as general counsel -- and both devoted their retirement years to the interests of SCORE.

The two were as unlike as two persons can be. Other than their nearly religious dedication to SCORE, about all they had in common was that each had been chairman of SCORE Chapter No. 1 in Washington, each had been Regional Representative in Region III, and each had come to SCORE from the federal bureaucracy -- Davidson from the Library of Congress and O'Rourke from various agencies including the Reconstruction Finance Corporation and the General Services Administration.

Davidson was not a tall man, but what he lacked in physical stature he more than made up in moral stature. O'Rourke wasn't all that physically tall either but he was taller than Davidson. Nonetheless, the two stood shoulder to shoulder in honesty and integrity.

Davidson's eyesight was poor and his hearing was not all that good either. He wore a hearing aid and thick glasses, and with the aid of a magnifying glass he would read the *Congressional Record* almost daily and knew more about what was happening on the Hill than some of the congressmen who were filling the pages of the *Record* with their wisdom.

O'Rourke didn't wear glasses; he didn't need them to see through bureaucratese.

Davidson was a mild and gentle man. O'Rourke had a vocabulary that would blister the paint off a filing cabinet all the way across the room. There is evidence, though, that he used his knowledge of a mule skinner's vernacular to cover a trace of tenderness. One day he and Davidson were having lunch together at Scholl's Cafeteria at McPherson Square in the nation's capital, and the fish Davidson ordered was stitched with bones.

"Goddam!" O'Rourke snorted. Then he proceeded to graphically trace the ancestry of the fish, the fisherman and the cook all the way back to the Cenozoic Age while he delicately removed the bones Davidson, with his poor eyesight, might fail to see.

Walter P. O'Rourke

Actually, O'Rourke had excellent command of the English language. The compendium he presented to the National SCORE Conference in 1972 on the legal status of the ACTION situation, while a trifle long and somewhat lawyerly, is an excellent example of his lucid logic. His logic, his command of the language, and his legal wisdom were to stand SCORE in good stead during the organization's middle years.

During the dying days of SCORE's association with ACTION, SCORE leaders were casting about for a way to prevent SCORE from ever again being tossed from one agency to another like a political football. Incorporation as a nonprofit, charitable association seemed to be the solution. This was reinforced by the fact the federal General Accounting Office had ruled that SCORE members were not federal employees, paid or otherwise. GAO's opinion later was enacted into law by Congress which split a hair in the process -- it ruled that SCORE members, while on official business, would be deemed the same as federal employees so they could come under the Federal Tort Claims Act.

The reasoning behind SCORE's plan to incorporate is simple. It's pretty well established that an employee, if he wants to stay employed, had better go where his boss sends him. If he is not an employee he can tell a presumptious boss where to go. If SCORE became a separate entity, SCORE leaders reasoned, SBA or Congress might be able to shift the SCORE program but would be unable to shift SCORE.

While SCORE leaders knew what should be done they were reluctant to take the step. As they talked and vacillated, Henry Warren, then Associate Administrator for Management Assistance, tipped the balance. During a conference with SCORE leaders on other matters, and not knowing their thinking, he suggested it might be a good idea if SCORE incorporated.

SCORE took that chance remark as approval. O'Rourke drew up the Articles of Incorporation, wrote the Bylaws, registered SCORE's trademark, and filed for income tax exemption with the Internal Revenue Service. Walter Channing recalls that Warren was not surprised by the action but was surprised by the speed with which it was accomplished. Channing, along with Jay Lansford, Joseph Knight and, of course, O'Rourke and Davidson, were the incorporators.

For the period SCORE was affiliated with ACTION, it tried to operate under a two-headed arrangement. Almost as soon as it was free from that entanglement it set up a two-headed arrangement of its own. Following the incorporation of the Service Corps of Retired Executives Association, the National SCORE Council continued to operate as SCORE's national contact with SBA while the Association handled corporate business. Boards of Directors of each were identical. This unwieldy arrangement continued until 1982 when the two national bodies were merged into the Association.

The middle years of SCORE produced vast changes in the organization; in addition to becoming a nonprofit, charitable association, a national office was established in Washington, D. C., ACE was merged into SCORE, and the system of District Representatives was started. All of the latter three transferred to SCORE volunteers administrative duties which previously had been handled by SBA employees.

The absorption of ACE by SCORE is quite typical; it was something SBA pressed upon SCORE for a number of years, but the formal merger was not accomplished until 1982.

SCORE's opposition to the merger of the two groups was more real than cosmetic. While the goals of the two groups are identical, the organizations are quite dissimilar. ACE, founded in 1968 during the brief tenure of Andrew Jank as director of SBA's Office of Management Assistance, was and is a group of persons still actively engaged in business. Originally, members were recruited by SBA, SBA made their assignments and handled their reports in much the same manner as SBA had tried, and failed, to handle SCORE three years earlier. Transferral of ACE to SCORE would give SCORE the task of handling ACE's paper work.

But there was more to SCORE's opposition than an increase in paper work. SCORE recruits, for example, are screened by SCORE, by SBA and, until recently, by the Federal Bureau of Investigation. ACE members did not have to go through this screening process, nor did they have to subscribe to SCORE's Code of Ethics.

The trend to view the two groups as one started early. When SCORE was transferred to ACTION, ACE went along. Even SCORE's testimony in Congress relative to the return of SCORE to SBA referred to the two programs as SCORE/ACE. But accomplishment of a real merger was not a simple thing. As O'Rourke pointed out in 1976, in another logical and lucid presentation to the SCORE Board of Directors, the absorption could not be accomplished without drastic changes in SCORE's Articles of Incorporation, its Bylaws and its Standard Operating Manual.

The creation of the District Representative position came about a little easier. The concept originated with SBA. Apparently two motives were involved -- one to bring SCORE together into a more cohesive organization, the other to save money for SBA by transferring more of SCORE's administration from SBA salaried personnel to volunteers.

At the time, SBA had 10 Regions and 65 Districts. The Regions and Districts were administered by Regional Administrators and District Directors. SCORE had but 10 Regional Representatives to oversee nearly 400 chapters. District Representatives, it was argued, would give SCORE counterparts to the District Directors in each District. However, unlike other SCORE officials who are elected, DRs would be appointed by RRs with the approval of SBA District Directors.

As originally conceived, the newly appointed DRs would need the seven-league boots Congress failed to provide the management assistance officers in SBA's early days. They were to be the chief communications link between the chapters and SBA's District Directors and SCORE's RRs, they were to be responsible for recruiting, training, public relations and the formation of chapters in their Districts, they were to be responsible for evaluation of chapter and member work, they were to serve on district and regional advisory councils and to attend district, regional and national SCORE meetings, they would organize, plan and conduct pre-business workshops, spend two days a week in the District Office conferring and working with the District Director and the RR, attend a minimum of four meetings a year of each chapter in the District and all of the meetings of the DR's home chapter, and serve as SCORE's advocate by speaking to interested groups in the District. It doesn't take much finger counting to determine that the DR, a volunteer, would be working five full days a week.

In an early memorandum discussing the creation of the DR position SBA admitted it did not have the manpower to properly administer SCORE, while pointing out that it was costing SBA more than $4 million a year for administration alone. The memorandum estimated that the DRs would save SBA between $1 million and $2 million a year.

With a growing organization that was to be more responsible for administering its own affairs, it became obvious SCORE needed a national office to serve the chapters, to promote SCORE and to provide leadership and tools for recruiting and training. The proposal for a national office came from SBA but was readily accepted by SCORE. Nonetheless, it took three long years to get the job done.

Four factors entered into the long negotiations, not the least of which was SCORE itself. SCORE was slow, perhaps even timid, about venturing onto that new ground. If anyone ever has tried to set up an office without the guidelines of prior experience, the difficulties are apparent. Office location. Space needed. Equipment. Duties, both for the office generally and for its staff. Criteria for selecting personnel. Job descriptions. Length of service for the volunteers. Where the volunteers would be housed. Need for and number of paid staff. Payment of volunteers' expenses.

Channing and Knight did most of this work with the help of Davidson and O'Rourke, both of whom lived in the Washington area. But the work was slow. Distance separated the four men. Most of their "conferring" was done by mail since none had access to the Federal Telecommunications System.

A second factor in the slow pace was the change from the Ford to the Carter Administration. Political appointees from one administration go out onto the job market while the new political appointees come on board. All the newcomers had to be brought up to running speed before plans for the SCORE office could be advanced.

A third factor was scandal -- not SCORE's but SBA's. SBA periodically has been wracked with one sort of scandal or another, and one was in progress while SCORE was trying to get its office door opened. It has been estimated that during the time SCORE was trying to find the proper door key, 75 per cent of SBA's office staff time was being devoted to damage control.

Patricia M. Cloherty, who came to SBA under the Carter Administration as Deputy SBA Administrator, said, "It's the squeaky wheel that gets the attention and, considering all the noise that was going on at the time, SCORE was not very squeaky and was not considered a problem."

Dr. Pat LeMay Burr, who replaced Warren as Associate Aministrator for Management Assistance, has another view. She said, "Bureaucrats are not anxious to do anything for the first time. The task of establishing space in a federal building for a private group seemed a lot more complicated to the bureaucrats than it did to the private sector."

Johnnie L. Albertson, a 15-year veteran of SBA and currently Deputy Associate Administrator for Minority Small Business and Capital Ownership Development, puts it more bluntly. "Bureaucracy is structured with rules, regulations and opinions from many sources," she says. "It is basically designed to inhibit a person from doing the job for which he was hired."

Ms. Albertson, who was director of the Office of Program Delivery during the formative years of the National SCORE Office, says this is the main reason it is so difficult to get answers from bureaucracy and to get jobs done.

An example. It was in March 1987 that SBA asked SCORE to consolidate three SBA publications into one pamphlet. Two SCORE members took on the chore in June, and by September, even though they lived several thousand miles apart, they had completed their task. Their consolidation crept through various SBA offices at 1441 L Street, N. W., Washington, D. C., for a year and a half before it became available.

There are 21 divisions or offices in SBA's central office in Washington. One of them is the Office of Business Development. On its own, BD has seven subdivisions. Not everything, of course, has to be run through all 28 "offices" at SBA, but many plans, proposals and innovations have to go through so many "In" baskets for opinions and suggestions the original proposal has whiskers on it by the time it gets back to its starting point.

The proposal for SCORE's national office, even though initially it came from SBA, had to run this gauntlet. Along the way there were meetings and conferences, and even though both Davidson and O'Rourke had come to SCORE from bureaucracy and knew its functionings, they were unable to speed the process.

There came a time, though, when just about everything seemed to be resolved. Everything, that is, except for the objections of SBA's legal department. It contended that SBA did not have the authority to set up an office for a quasi public, or a private, organization.

There was some validity in this position. It was made a non-issue, however, when SCORE was granted $40,000 by the J. Howard Pew Freedom Trust to be used as "seed" money to get the office open.

The legal department, however, was not to be put off so easily. It then declared that SBA did not have the money to pay NSO expenses once the office was open. It was Dr. Burr who spoiled that argument -- she took the money from another source and applied it to NSO. Dr. Burr, who now is a professor of marketing at Incarna College in San Antonio, Texas, says that finding the money for NSO was her only real contribution to the establishment of the office.

Even with the money available, the legal department was not to be deterred. It then raised the question of need for a national SCORE office, something that had been decided in the early discussions over the establishment of the office -- a focal point to provide services and support to the increasing number of chapters which also were expanding the scope of their activities. One of the main goals was to provide counseling training tools for SCORE members. It was upon this latter point that SBA lawyers hung their argument: Since SCORE members were retired business executives, the lawyers said, they needed no further training.

Channing, Simon and others met all one day at SBA headquarters, trying to convince SBA lawyers that the training involved was not business training but training in counseling; but the meeting ended at 4:30 p.m., still deadlocked. Ms. Cloherty, who now is an associate with Alan Patricos & Associates in New York City, met with the lawyers that evening, and the following morning she announced that the roadblocks had been removed and that the SCORE office could be opened in space at SBA headquarters in Washington.

That was 10 years ago and today Ms. Cloherty cannot recall what log she pulled to eliminate the logjam.

Early in 1978 a formal agreement was signed by SBA and the SCORE Association, and leases were signed with the owners of an apartment building in Silver Spring, Maryland, to provide housing for the volunteer directors who would serve at NSO. Jack H. Ducate was the first executive director, Bryson Randolph the first public relations director, and Cecelia F. Stanton the first membership and training director.

The office, located on the ground floor of the SBA building, was small and tucked away behind some other SBA offices. The air conditioning worked in winter and the heating system in summer. The furniture could only be described as Goodwill discards. Wastebaskets never were emptied on a regular schedule.

There were two typewriters in the office when it opened -- one for the secretary/receptionist, the other a spare in case the first one broke down. One executive director refused to let anyone touch the second typewriter, claiming that business executives do not need typewriters; typewriters were for secretaries. When the director's three-month tour of duty was over and before his replacement could put a new embargo on the machine, the public relations director laid claim to the spare, setting a precedent that eventually would provide enough typewriters to go around.

SCORE learned almost immediately that three-month tours for volunteer directors were much too short; volunteers barely had time to learn their way around before it was time to leave. Terms were extended to six months and then to a year if volunteers could be found who were willing to leave their homes for extended periods.

Work at NSO expanded rapidly, not only as new director positions were added (e.g., international trade) but also as additional duties were assigned to it by SBA. In the process, the office has become computerized. There are now two full time computer operators in the office. The SAVANT, which operates independently of NSO but in NSO space, has its own computer to publish SCORE's monthly news journal.

Julius Davidson

Even before the advent of the computers, though, NSO outgrew its space at SBA headquarters and moved briefly to a store-front office on 15th Street, N. W. before moving in early 1983 to the Board of Trade building on 20th Street, N. W. Just before Christmas 1988 the office was moved again to larger quarters in the Metropolitan Square building at 655 15th Street, N. W. A reasonably permanent address, however, may not be in the cards. NSO may lose its current lease and may have to move again.

Another problem that has bugged NSO from the beginning has been a matter of staff continuity. With directors serving short terms their programs tended to be jumpy. The only continuity that was provided was through Davidson and O'Rourke and the salaried office administrator. This has now changed. The executive directorship is now salaried, as is the position of editor of The SAVANT.

In the early days of the office Davidson took it upon himself to try to guide the volunteer directors through the intricacies of bureaucracy.

"You have to learn to think like bureaucrats if you expect to deal with them," he advised.

Exactly what he meant by that he never explained but there are clues. For example, the volunteers came from the business world and it is the job of a business person to make money. The job of a bureaucrat is to spend money. A business person is supposed to wind up his year with more money in the bank than he had when he started; a bureaucrat is supposed to wind up his year broke. If an agency has any money left over at the end of a fiscal year, the money has to go back to the federal treasury. Bureaucracy doesn't like that. If it fails to use all of its appropriation in any year, bureaucrats reason, it would be difficult to ask for an increase in its appropriation for the upcoming year.

Davidson understood this.

Back in 1980 SBA directed NSO to produce a series of television commercials to advertise SCORE. The NSO staff argued that the machinery for distributing the series had not been set up and that there was no way to track the effectiveness of the program.

It was close to the end of the fiscal year and SBA said, "The money's there. Use it. We don't want it to go back to the federal treasury."

Davidson sided with SBA. "That's the way bureaucracy works," he explained. "If you have the money, spend it. Otherwise your funding may be reduced next year."

The television commercials were produced and some of them are still in use. But to this day no one really knows how effective they have been.

"As I look at the sea of wisdom and talent around me, if I didn't have such an enormous ego I'd get an inferiority complex."

Overheard during a coffee break at the
National SCORE Workshop in
San Diego, California, in 1987

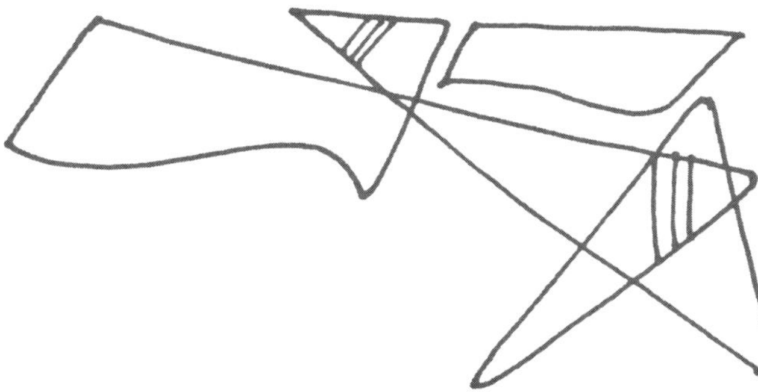

Chapter 6

Paper Work and Other Goodies

(Like Benson and Sebastian, Engelman and Powers are not real. But they could be.)

Hub Benson dropped into the chair beside Sid Engelman's desk in the SBA District Office. Sid was a retired accountant, a five-year SCORE member, bald and overweight. He looked at Benson over the top of his glasses and tossed his pen onto the pile of paper in front of him.

"No," he said. "Whatever it is you're going to ask, the answer is no."

Benson grinned. "What makes you think I'm going to ask something?"

"Ever since we elected you chapter chairman all you've done is ask questions. I don't think there's a declarative sentence in you."

"That bad, huh?"

"See! There you go again. Another question."

"If I'm that bad why did you keep reelecting me chairman?"

It was Sid's turn to grin. "You walked into that one. We kept electing you chairman because no one else would take the job." Then he turned serious. "No, that's not fair," he admitted. "We kept electing you because you were doing a good job. You let us down, though, when you resigned to take the DR job. And saddled me with the chairmanship and all this paper work." He waved his hand at the pile on his desk.

"You can't blame me for that, Sid. You volunteered."

Engleman pushed his glasses up on his nose. "Volunteered, hell! You knew when you nominated me no one else would take the job. You didn't even have a vice chairman! That's one of the things that's wrong with this outfit. Everybody wants to be an Indian. No chiefs. As for me, I'd rather be playing golf."

"You haven't played golf in five years."

"That doesn't mean I wouldn't if I didn't have to sit behind a postage stamp desk putting pencil marks in little boxes!"

Benson leaned back in his chair, pressed his fingertips together, and looked at the ceiling. "If I recall, Sid, I interviewed you when you applied for membership. I remember what you said. You said,

'I need something to do! I've played so much golf it's no longer any fun to cheat. I've caught so many fish the neighbors lock their doors when they see me coming. And I've traveled so much I'm convinced that airlines are the Twentieth Century's version of medieval torture.' "

"That's pretty good. Did I say that?"

"You sure did."

"Hmmm. But that doesn't change anything. I...," he began and Benson chimed in. Together they said, "I didn't join SCORE to do paper work."

They both laughed.

"Seriously, how'd we let ourselves get into this mess?" Sid asked.

Benson twisted around in his chair and crossed his legs.

"Evolution," he replied. "Evolution that began more than 20 years ago when SBA discovered it couldn't afford the SCORE program unless the volunteers handled some of their own paper work. To give the devil his due, SBA was caught in a bind. Congress mandated that SBA give management assistance to small business but failed to provide the manpower to do the job. SCORE was SBA's solution. But the stars in SBA's eyes at the time got in the way of reality. SBA failed to reckon that a program, even one where the people work for nothing, needs administration. And administration costs money. SBA's solution has been to turn more administration, more leadership, more paper work over to volunteers who didn't volunteer for that line of work. That has caused a lot of resentment on the part of SCORE members all across the country."

"You can say that again. It appears that the bind SBA has been in has been panned off on SCORE. Not enough of the right people in the right places."

Benson agreed. "Something like that. And SCORE hasn't been doing a very good job of it. For the most part it has been counting potatoes. Counting number of chapters, number of members, number of clients, number of workshops. But nothing about what all that activity has produced."

"Aw, I wouldn't say that. What about all those big name companies SCORE helped when they were just getting started?"

"Of course, there have been successes. Some of them pretty outstanding, too. But if all we can tick off are a couple of dozen big name companies out of a couple of million clients in the last 20 years, you can't say SCORE has had an enviable record."

Sid picked up his pen and threw it down again. It rolled off the desk onto the floor. "You're talking nonsense!" he charged. "There have been hundreds -- no, thousands -- of businesses that we've helped."

Benson leaned back in his chair. "You just proved my point. There probably have been hundreds of thousands of people that we've helped but our records don't show it. We have no idea how many jobs our efforts have created, or how many additional tax dollars we've generated. And that's becoming increasingly important. If SCORE is to continue to get funding -- from SBA, direct from Congress, or from some other source -- it is going to have to prove that it really is doing what, for years, it's been saying it's doing."

Sid bent over to pick up his pen, but his girth got in his way. Benson retrieved the ball point and laid it on the desk. "That's one area in which the Small Business Development Centers have it over SCORE like a tent. They have facts and figures to back up their claims."

"Sure they do," Sid countered. "But they have paid personnel to do what SBA expects a bunch of volunteers to do for nothing. It costs SBDC 30 to 40 times as much to counsel a client as it does SCORE."

Benson nodded. "That's right. But look at it this way. SBDC can readily admit it costs a couple of thousand dollars to counsel a client because it can also say the counseling generated X number of jobs that created an additional payroll of so many millions of dollars a year. It can say that tax revenues increased by a specific amount. And it can prove that a neighborhood has been improved through their efforts. That's quite a return for a couple of thousand dollars investment. That's the kind of music Congressmen like to hear. SCORE doesn't have the proper manpower and, yes, even the willingness to match that.

About all it can do is to count the number of people it has talked to. There's no comparison!"

Lee Powers stuck his head around the movable partition that marked Sid's office. "Hey!" he announced. "You guys will never believe the case I just had!"

Sid consulted the assignment log. "The delicatessen. The one that wouldn't tell us what the problem was."

"Yep, that's the one," Lee said. Powers was a man of about average height but it would have taken two of him to cast a respectable shadow in bright sunlight. He had a shock of white hair that was molded and styled, and his clothing always reflected the latest trends. Until floored by a heart attack he had been the owner of a very successful advertising agency. After triple-bypass surgery he had sold his business and joined SCORE. Recently he had expanded his activities to include teaching a class in marketing at the local community college.

"You should have seen that couple," Powers continued. "She's Swiss, short, chubby, apple cheeked and cute; just the kind whose picture you'd expect to see on a five-pound box of Swiss chocolates. He's Austrian, tall, almost as skinny as I am, dour, humorless and so disciplined he squeaks when he walks. They sell all kinds of goodies -- luncheon meat, cheese, candy, pastries. You name it. They served me a cup of hot chocolate that was so thick and creamy you could spread it on a slice of bread."

"What's their problem?" Sid asked.

"You know, I had a little trouble getting that out of them. They brought out their books for me to go over. Their bookkeeping system wasn't elaborate but it worked for them. But when I saw their bank book I almost choked on the hot chocolate. It was in six figures, to the left of the decimal point!"

Benson whistled. "All that in a checking account?"

"No. Savings account. The checking account only had a couple of hundred bucks in it. It turned out that the savings account was their problem."

"Ah," Sid said. "Investments. I hope you advised them to see an investment counselor or a broker."

"Nope, I didn't do that since investing was not the problem. Philosophy was their problem. He's of the Old World. He feels that people should work -- and that includes his three sons who work at the store after school and weekends for nothing -- and all the money should be socked away. No money should be spent unless it's for absolute necessities. She's of the Old World, too, but America has changed her. She wants her sons to play in sports, she wants to belong to the PTA and, most of all, she wants some furniture in her house that isn't second hand. Now, how's that for a problem?

"They weren't communicating," Benson observed.

"Oh, they were communicating all right. They were doing fine. They hate each other."

"What did you do?" Sid asked.

"I advised them to get a divorce."

Benson and Engelman sat upright in their chairs. "You what?" Benson demanded.

"Migod!" Sid exploded. "We're business counselors, not marriage counselors! We could get into a pack of trouble!"

Powers was unruffled. "Oh, I don't think so. What I did was to give some business partners some advice. Split. The fact they're married has nothing to do with it." Then he grinned. "Besides, they already had decided on my solution. All they wanted was a second opinion and someone to go over their settlement agreement to see if it was fair. From a business standpoint, you understand."

His listeners relaxed. Benson heaved a heavy sigh. "You know, Lee, I think maybe you belong in the Solomon class. I don't know what I would have done had I been in your place. But that word 'divorce' scares me. Let's make sure it doesn't appear in the case report. That smacks too much of marriage rather than business counseling."

Sid shrugged. "O. K.," he said, "but I don't think it would make any difference. I doubt if anyone ever reads any of these reports after they leave this office."

Benson turned to Powers. "Just before you came in, Lee," he said, "we were talking about SBDC.

With your connections at the community college you must have rubbed shoulders with some of their people in the branch office there. I think you once told me you had helped them on a couple of cases. What's your opinion of SBDC?"

"Funny you should ask that. Just the other day I got my hands on a copy of the testimony of a man by the name of Warren -- Henry Warren, I think it was. He was some sort of an SBA wheel back in Washington. He testified before the Senate Small Business Committee on the establishment of SBDC. The way he outlined it, it wasn't such a bad idea. SBDC was supposed to become a sort of extension service for business -- something like Agriculture's Extension Service for farmers. You know, a place where research would be conducted. Demographic surveys made. Things like that. It also was originally designed to pull together all groups -- federal, state, local or private -- that were working to help small business. That way a small business person could get the help he needed in one place instead of having to run around to a lot of offices. Of course, that's not the way it turned out."

Benson agreed. "I've heard that SBA stubbed its toe right in the beginning; that it not only failed to tell SCORE there was going to be a new kid on the block but also failed to inform some of its own Regional Administrators a new program was heading in their direction. I can understand SBA's failure to tell

SCORE. Even though SBA and SCORE have an agreement that SBA will inform SCORE of any changes in programs or policies that may affect SCORE, the agreement has been honored more in the breach than in the execution. But I can't understand how SBA failed to keep its field informed of a change that was to be as sweeping as SBDC."

"I hadn't heard that," Powers replied, "but that doesn't mean it isn't so. As I get the picture from the Warren testimony, SBDC was to be the big picture while everything else, including SCORE, would be simply parts of it."

"Didn't SBDC make another run at trying to take over the entire program a few years ago?" Engelman asked.

Benson nodded. "In 1981, I think it was. SBDC, which has a lobbying office in Washington, made a pitch to Congress to take over SBA's entire management assistance program. Congress didn't buy it, but the move must have thrown a scare into both SBA and SCORE."

"Had it worked," Powers added, "it probably would have put SBDC about in the position envisioned by that Warren guy in his testimony four years earlier."

Sid posed a question. "From what you've been saying here, Lee, I get the impression you have a high opinion of SBDC."

Powers chewed his lower lip. "Let's get a couple of things straight here. What I said was that I thought the concept of an extension service for small business sounded like a good idea. I don't recall saying a thing about how SBDC is operating. Now if you want my opinion on that, I'll tell you it's not living up to its potential; it's spending entirely too much time doing one-on-one small business counseling. SBDC is not supposed to be just another counseling service -- it's supposed to be wide ranging. There. Have I put you straight?"

Sid nodded. "I hear you," he said. "And what you've said simply reinforces my feeling that SCORE and SBDC are in competition."

"In a sense, that's true," Powers admitted, then added, "SCORE and SBDC are not very much alike. SBDC's vision is supposed to be broad. SCORE's is relatively narrow; it focuses primarily on one-on-one counseling and workshops. SBDC gets its money -- and it's a wad -- from Congress through SBA. SCORE gets its stipend from SBA, a part of SBA's appropriation. SBDC's people are salaried. SCORE's people, except for seven or eight in the National SCORE Office and the people hired in the chapters to do secretarial work, are volunteers."

"Whoa!" Benson cut in. "Chapter clerical support people are not SCORE employees. For the most part they work for various manpower agencies with which SCORE has contracts."

Powers shrugged. "Whatever. The fact remains that SBDC, in spite of its high budget, does not have the qualified manpower to compete with SCORE in counseling activities. It's outgunned. To really compete with SCORE for counseling cases it would have to do one of three things: Get a lot bigger budget to hire a lot more people, get SCORE's full cooperation, or organize its own cadre of volunteers." He looked at his watch. "Hey, I've got to go or I'll be late for my marketing class out at the college."

He started to leave but Sid stopped him. "Your report. You haven't made out your report."

"Damned paper work! I'll make it out the next time I'm in the office." He waved his hand and departed.

"There we go again," Sid said. "Damned paper work. It'll probably be a week before I see him again." He sighed. "He seems to know a lot about SBDC."

Benson nodded. "I imagine he spends some time with various members of the SBDC staff at the college. That bit about cooperation between SCORE and SBDC bothers me some. 'Cooperation' is a word that can have as many meanings as there are people using it. In some cases where SCORE has cooperated too well, SCORE has all but disappeared. In other instances where there has been little cooperation, the two are throwing spitballs at each other. There are times when I feel SCORE is having an identity crisis."

He stood up. "I'd better go," he announced. Got some errands to run. Finish your paper work, Sid." He started to walk away, then turned back.

"Hey," he announced, "I almost forgot. I was going to ask you something."

Sid rolled his eyes. "I knew it! I knew there was something on your mind. Okay, out with it. What's on your mind this time?"

"I want some advice." He avoided Sid's eyes and looked out the window. "I'm thinking about running for Regional Representative. What do you think?"

Engelman's face lit up. "Say! That's great. You'd make a great RR!"

Benson turned and faced Sid. "Thanks, Sid. But there's more."

"Oh?"

"Yes. If I'm elected I'm going to appoint you District Representative. You spend too much time sitting behind that desk. You should get out and around more." He paused, then added, "Maybe get out and play a little golf."

He turned and walked away, grinning. If Sid did the job as Benson expected he would, he wouldn't have much time for golf.

"We sit around debating what we have to do, agree on what's to be done, and then do nothing."

Herbert J. L. Baum, Past President,
National SCORE Association,
during an interview in 1988

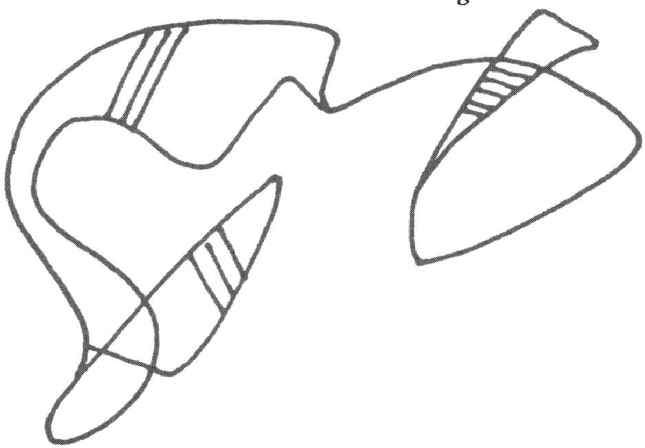

Chapter 7

Problems

Ever since its beginning 25 years ago SCORE has been beset by a variety of continuous problems. They're easy to spot. Proper screening of applicants for membership. Maintaining a qualified cadre. Proper assignment of cases. No reports and/or inadequate reports. Lack of follow-ups. Lack of counselor training. Lack of quality control.

As continuous as these problems have been, they have been just as continuously attacked. And with some success. But they never go away; they continue to lurk on the sidelines, ready to erupt at any time. Some of this can be attributed to SCORE's ever-changing membership. With the generally accepted attrition rate of 20 per cent a year, SCORE probably has had between 30,000 and 40,000 members since October 5, 1964. Each new member has to be made aware of the lurking problems and instructed in how to avoid them.

The presence of the problems was discovered early. Dr. Moon listed most of them in his study on the early days of SCORE. In 1979 SBA commissioned the Rockville (Maryland) Consulting Group to study the SCORE operation. It reached pretty much the same conclusions. In 15 years the problems were as healthy and as vigorous as they had been in the beginning.

At about the same time as the Rockville report was being released, Johnnie Albertson, then director of SBA's Office of Program Delivery, took the SCORE Board of Directors to task. She charged that there were two SCOREs, the field on the one hand and the administration on the other. In a rough paraphrase of Kipling, what she said was that the twain wasn't jibing too well.

Ms. Albertson is not too popular with some in the SCORE organization; they feel that she would just as soon see the SCORE organization, as distinguished from the field, disappear. Now Deputy Associate Administrator for Minority Small Business and Capital Ownership Development, she said in a recent interview that SCORE has not yet reached its potential because the national organization has failed to provide the proper leadership.

Shortly after her verbal criticism to the SCORE Board of Directors, her office announced that the National SCORE Office might be closed in 30 days. NSO was instructed to submit to SBA an evaluation of its operation with emphasis on the value of the office to

SBA and on the quality, quantity and pertinence of its output and acceptance and utilization in the field.

SCORE appointed a committee of four Board members to make the evaluation. It produced a 48-page report that, since NSO still is in existence, apparently dispelled SBA's concerns. One area in which SBA wanted proof was the existence of a network to achieve a well informed, unified, and more efficiently organized membership.

George A. Breffeilh of Lake Charles, Louisiana, Regional Representative from Region VI and later President of the SCORE Association, responded in this way in the report:

> The responsibilities of NSO should terminate when it prepares an opinion, develops a program or organizes a function. The execution of the procedure, program or function is the responsibility which extends from the RRs, through the DRs and chapter chairmen to the counselor....The chairmen are not prepared to act upon the information because of a breakdown in, or lack of line communication between, the staff office and the chapter chairmen -- the responsibilities of the RRs and the DRs.

This appraisal tacitly admits the established system had not been working and that the fault was a breakdown in communications between NSO and the field. As originally conceived, NSO was to be a staff function -- it would produce material under the direction of the Board of Directors but it was up to the RRs and the DRs to make effective use of what NSO produced. This was the defect to which Breffeilh alluded.

To help bridge the gap between the field and the national office, Breffeilh devised the activity reporting system now in universal use throughout SCORE, a major contribution not readily appreciated. The system has provided the basis for the current management reporting techniques.

Lawrence R. Rosenbaum, while director of SBA's Office of Planning and Budget, in his 1984 survey of the SCORE operation, spotted the same defect to which Breffeilh alluded. His suggested remedy was to change NSO from a staff to a line function, thereby providing a more direct line of communications between national SCORE and the field and, in the process, relieving RRs and DRs of some of their administrative responsibilities.

Much of Rosenbaum's survey and report was based upon the report of a 1983 Task Force set up jointly by SCORE and SBA to "examine SCORE, study ways to improve it, and prepare a plan to obtain the highest level of organizational efficiency."

By its nature, the Task Force report was laced with criticism, and among them were the old bugaboos of poor screening of applicants for membership, poor training of counselors, viewing chapters as social groups, poor reporting, lackadaisical approach to matching counselor skills with client needs, lack of follow-up and analysis of results.

The SCORE Board of Directors, for the most part, rejected the recommendations of the Task Force, primarily on the grounds they were too "structured." And perhaps they were. But that did not negate the validity of the Task Force's findings. The perennial problems continued to exist.

James C. Sanders, former SBA Administrator, recently looked back on his four years with SBA and observed, "SCORE's effectiveness could be improved with quality members, proper assignments to match clients with counselors' skills, and evaluation of work. The quality of SCORE work and the quality of some of its members is questionable. There is no discipline in SCORE; the organization has a great need for self policing."

Another problem, as he sees it, has been in SCORE's failure to evaluate its work.

"Mismatching and failure to evaluate work have produced too many negative results," he said. "SCORE and SBA can't expect 100 per cent positive results, but there have been altogether too many negative results."

He criticized counselor training, pointing out that too many members are unskilled or untrained in the art of leading a client through the problems of self employment and the pitfalls of owning one's own business. And he guessed that 50 per cent of SCORE's membership is deadwood, unqualified, or made up of those who view SCORE as a social organization.

Like Ms. Albertson, he differentiated between SCORE counselors in the field and SCORE members who have moved into leadership positions. He charged that SCORE's top echelon "tilted at too many windmills and made mountains out of molehills" instead of tackling basic problems.

What Sanders did in his latter-day criticism was to reiterate many of SCORE's problems of the last 25 years. It is not as though SCORE has been unaware of, or has failed to tackle, these internal problems; on the contrary, SCORE's leadership has made repeated runs at them, individually and collectively. Yet they seem to remain as intractable as ever.

There has to be a reason.

One possible answer may be that the problems are not many but one. Both Sanders and Ms. Albertson alluded to this in their recent appraisals of SCORE leadership. And there are in SCORE those who see leadership as the means to drain the swamp, thereby getting rid of the alligators.

The idea of improved leadership is not a new one. As far back as 1975 Henry Warren, then SBA's Associate Administrator for Management Assistance, told the National SCORE Council that SCORE was becoming more the operator of its own functions and that the possibility of a permanent SCORE staff should be considered in order to perform many of the needed functional controls of the SCORE program.

Since then a number of proposals have been advanced, some of them far-reaching. One of the first to call for sweeping change was introduced by James G. Black, then chairman of the San Diego, California, Chapter No. 140, at the National SCORE Workshop in Omaha in 1978. Black's speech, in somewhat archaic terminology, was a stemwinder. It was about counselors and the standards of excellence that are expected of them. It touched on morality, on ethics, on empathy, on dedication, and wound up with a call for leadership to "make certain that the proper emphasis and direction are given to the selection, motivation and training of SCORE members."

Black was well suited to deliver that speech. He holds a Ph.D. in economics and is a retired one-star general of the U. S. Army. He taught in army management schools and was a professor of economics at the National War College.

Black started his business career as a regional auditor for an insurance company. When World War II broke out he enlisted in the army as a private, attended Officer Candidate School, and was sent overseas to the Pacific Theater as a captain. When he returned to the United States in 1946 he elected to stay in the military and was attached to the Office of Comptroller General. In 1953 the army sent him to Georgetown University to study for his doctorate in economics. He retired from the army in 1962 and went to work for Battelle Memorial Institute, retiring a second time in 1972. The following year he joined the San Diego SCORE chapter.

His long career in active service is evident; he walks with a military bearing. His doctorate is not so apparent except in his ability to reduce a discussion to its least common denominator and to produce a logical solution. But he is also pragmatic; he realizes that logic is not always the complete solution, especially when it runs up against emotion.

The same year he delivered the Omaha speech he was elected Regional Representative in Region IX and at the National SCORE Workshop in Tulsa in 1979 he proposed that a leadership program be developed for SCORE. The Board of Directors adopted his proposal and Black put together a plan that would enable SCORE to select, nurture, train and assign selected SCORE members in a progressive manner to build a reservoir of future SCORE leaders. The plan was sent to all chapter chairmen whose responsibility it was to launch the program locally.

The plan, for lack of implementation at the local level, fell by the wayside. The reason is obvious -- lack of leadership to start a leadership program.

Today, Black is somewhat disillusioned over the failure of the Executive Development Program. "At times," he said recently, "it appears as though SCORE is trying to self destruct. It is not a social organization. It needs self discipline. Business is changing, becoming more complex. This is SCORE's challenge in the future and it will take discipline to meet that challenge. SCORE needs a different type of

James G. Black

leadership vis-a-vis the changing, complex business world."

Black, who has resigned from SCORE to work with the legislative committee of the American Association of Retired Persons, served as President of the national organization, following Herbert J. L. Baum, another Regional Representative in Region IX. After his terms as President were over Baum suggested a different approach to the leadership problem -- he proposed a business plan for SCORE, something with which all business executives are familiar, as the vehicle to produce leadership. The plan Baum devised touched upon recruiting for quality rather than numbers, matching counselor skills with client needs, increased in-depth counseling, and appraisals of counseling effectiveness. While it was approved by the Board of Directors and sent to the field for implementation, it suffered the same fate as Black's Executive Development Program. To Baum's knowledge, the plan never was implemented, nor was there any follow-up at the national level.

"The problems we had at the time," he said recently, "are still with us."

Baum came to SCORE in 1971 after retiring from business in 1969. In between retirement and joining SCORE he took a sea voyage to the Far East on a freighter. Finding time heavy on his hands during long periods at sea, he wrote a small book on credit and collections. He had it published when he returned to

Herbert J. L. Baum

San Francisco and, to his surprise, sales more than paid for his long voyage.

Baum, who retired as president of a small manufacturing firm, rose rapidly in the SCORE organization, becoming Regional Representative in 1975 and President of the national organization in 1979. He did this while under a severe physical handicap -- arthritis. Since then he has undergone hip operations and has, from outward appearances at least, fully recovered.

His two terms as President of SCORE were not easy ones. It was during his tenure that emotions were running high among SCORE members over what they considered as inroads by SBDC into SCORE's territory.

"There was a division on the Board of Directors," Baum said, "over what to do about SBDCs. Some wanted SCORE to have nothing to do with SBDCs; others wanted to work with them. My view was that SBDC was a fact of life and that we should try to work in full partnership with them."

His position was somewhat between the other views and consequently was not exactly popular with either. Nonetheless, a policy statement was adopted.

"Real SCORE progress seems to elude us," Baum said in a recent interview. "As small business has enlarged its share of the nation's economy, SCORE's assistance has declined. Many past opportunities to become the most authoritative voice in small business counseling have evaporated for lack of initiative, drive and a predominantly laissez-faire attitude. Inevitably, a continuation of this condition will lead to self destruction. To survive, SCORE must initiate strong measures to tighten our organization. Guidelines must come from the SCORE Association, action from the chapter level. There is an urgent need to prepare our leaders for their roles. The time is past when we should elect chapter chairmen on the basis of their willingness to serve or because of popular appeal. We know our failings. We sit around debating what we have to do, agree on what's to be done, and then do nothing."

When Baum's tenure on the Board was over, as a measure of his chapter's esteem for him, the chapter was renamed the "Herbert Baum SCORE Chapter No. 10." SBA has provided him with desk space in its Regional Office and he carries the title of "Regional SCORE Adviser." Currently he is chairman of the San Francisco cadre of counselors who work with delinquent borrowers, not as bill collectors, but as counselors trying to get the businesses back on their feet.

Both Black's Executive Development Program and Baum's Three-Year Business Plan were aimed at improving the administration of SCORE, and both failed for lack of implementation. Richard D. Lee of St. Petersburg, Florida, had two cracks at the problem, but both were turned down by the Board of

Directors. Parts of each, however, have been translated into reality.

Lee is a tall, big-boned man with an impish glint in his eyes, a quick smile and a booming laugh. But the glint can turn to steel, the smile to a frown and the laugh to a growl. Like Baum, he is afflicted with arthritis which has impaired his activity in recent years.

He is a retired Air Force colonel, having served as a logistics officer in just about every place where Air Force planes take off and land. He got in on the ground floor of the computer age and his thorough knowledge of the machines was tapped repeatedly when computers were being installed at NSO. Much of his time now is spent in the computer room in his waterfront St. Petersburg home, keeping current on the rapidly moving computer age.

He joined SCORE in 1974 when he retired from the Air Force, held about every office and committee chairmanship his chapter had to offer and served four and a half years as the first District Representative in the Miami District. He was elected Regional Representative in 1981 and served two terms. He now is a member of the SCORE Advisory Council.

Lee was a real working RR. He assiduously traveled his Region, the largest in the SCORE organization, and learned much about chapters' ability or inability to perform. He was not impressed. He found one chapter that met regularly, not to help small

Richard D. Lee

business but to play pinochle. He lifted the chapter's charter so fast the players even lost their meld.

His travels convinced him that chapters could not perform their functions without better administration. His solution was to devise and implement a chapter accreditation system designed to improve their management and, by adopting annual business plans with objectives capable of reasonable results, to weed out unproductive members. By and large the system worked; it improved chapter management and produced a high degree of uniformity among the chapters in his Region.

He explained to the Board of Directors what he had done and moved that an accreditation plan be adopted nationwide.

The motion was rejected.

"I can only guess at the reason," he admitted recently. "I think it was turned down because of the amount of work involved to set it up and administer it. Perhaps too much work to expect of volunteers."

His accreditation system also carried a system of chapter awards. SCORE now has a Chapter of the Year program, based in part upon the award system Lee devised for his Region IV accreditation program.

When the joint SBA/SCORE Task Force was set up to "examine SCORE, study ways to improve it and to prepare a plan to obtain the highest level of organizational self-sufficiency," Lee was named chairman. He spent a year with his six team members and submitted a report to SCORE and SBA near the end of 1983.

While the reorganization plan was rejected, a number of its recommendations have since been implemented. The National SCORE Office now has a paid executive director, NSO is moving more into line functions, and a number of small chapters, because of their inability to perform needed management functions, have opted to become satellites of nearby larger chapters.

All three of these programs -- Black's, Baum's and Lee's -- were aimed at the same thing -- improvement in the management of SCORE from the chapter level to the national organization. And even though neither of Lee's efforts received Board of Directors sanction, it is more than likely they are having a greater impact upon SCORE than the other two.

Lee thinks the basic solution to the problem or problems lies in the proper management of volunteers.

"SCORE," he says, "is one of the largest volunteer organizations in the country but it is lowest in volunteer management know-how. SCORE needs an extraordinary degree of leadership to manage volunteers and it doesn't have it. Most volunteer groups have leaders trained in volunteer management. SCORE does not. SCORE should send its leaders to short term volunteer management training schools. The cost would be small. The results would be great."

The theme keeps repeating itself. Jay Lansford said it at a meeting of the National SCORE Council in 1976. Deadwood. Upgrading chapters. Poor recruiting. Opposition to paper work. Rosenbaum said it again eight years later in his study of the SCORE organization. Accreditation of chapters. Better recruiting and better counseling training. Leaders need to be trained in volunteer management. Change the National SCORE Office function from staff to line.

That last one is a somewhat obscure point and needs elaboration. Through the years the Boards of both the National SCORE Council and the National SCORE Association have made many decisions affecting the management of the organization, and some of them never went any farther than the paper on which they were recorded. Black's Executive Development Program is one. Baum's Three-Year Business Plan is another. A decision to add three directors from outside of SCORE to the national Board to provide fresh ideas from outside the organization is still another. Hiring an archivist in the national office to get the organization's pile of paper in order, to keep them in order, and to prevent Board decisions from dropping into cracks is a decision that has been on the books for years.

In the past the Board has depended upon its members, as Regional Representatives, to enforce decisions in the field. It hasn't worked. There have been instances where RRs, having voted against a Board decision, have refused or neglected to enforce the decision in their Regions.

In the light of all this, Rosenbaum's recommendation makes sense, and gradually it is coming to pass. Changing the position of executive director at NSO from volunteer to salaried has added a sense of continuity long lacking in an organization that loses 20 per cent of its members every year.

"Talent is developed in retirement; character is formed in the rush of the world."

Goethe

Chapter 8

Seven Crises

Skill and wisdom were not Minerva's only attributes. She also was the goddess of defense. This has been fortunate. It has been fortunate because SCORE, in its 25-year span, has had to defend itself in seven crises, all generated by SBA. Three have been resolved; the remainder need more work.

All through their relationship, SCORE and SBA have been plowing new fields -- a group of private citizens doing continuous volunteer service for a federal agency -- and glitches have been bound to occur. At times, though, the relationship has been studded with something more than glitches; it has taken on the appearance of a spavined mule trying to pull a dull plow through a field of boulders.

It must be assumed that there was nothing venal in any SBA actions that created crises for SCORE. SCORE is too important to SBA. Without a payroll that would give the Office of Management and Budget a new set of peptic ulcers, SCORE is the only way SBA can deliver on the congressional mandate to counsel small business.

It must be assumed, too, that SBA, while taking actions that happened to produce crises for SCORE, took the actions with the well-being of the agency in mind. Whether actual improvement resulted is debatable, but few bureaucrats will intentionally take action that will endanger their agency or their jobs. There are apparent exceptions, of course. Charles W. Heatherly, who was SBA's acting Administrator during part of the Reagan Administration, is believed to have been participating in the attempt to scuttle SBA.

There is still another assumption that really isn't an assumption at all but an established fact: SCORE's defense in crisis time has resulted in a stronger and more mature organization.

Here are the seven crises:

TRANSFER TO SBA'S LOAN DIVISION -- This was SCORE's first crisis and it temporarily changed the character of SCORE from business counseling to bill collecting. It started in 1971 and ended in 1973, but in that two years approximately 50 per cent of SCORE's membership either resigned or became inactive. For a long period of time thereafter SCORE barely touched delinquent loan cases. In recent years this attitude has been relaxed and a few chapters have set up special groups of counselors to work with delinquent borrowers to try to get them current. An outstanding example of this is in the San Francisco District.

TRANSFER TO ACTION -- This crisis came close to spelling the end of SCORE. As with the transfer to the loan division, the transfer to ACTION was an attempt to change the character of SCORE, this time from economic to sociological. It, too, came in 1971 and did not end until 1975. This crisis, though, resulted in a benefit; it precipitated the formation of the SCORE Association which makes it difficult to bounce SCORE around like a football.

NATIONAL SCORE OFFICE -- This crisis is in two parts. Or perhaps two and a half, although the half never developed beyond the suggestion stage. The first part of the crisis was in the long period of time it took to establish the office after initial agreement had been reached.

The second part of the crisis came in 1981 when funding for the office was threatened. A study was made of the effectiveness of the office, and the crisis went away.

The one-half, the crisis that never developed, came from Denver in Region VIII in the form of a proposal from Ted Lindhorn, Assistant Regional

Administrator, and Ray Dowdle, Assistant District Director for Management Assistance. They proposed that management of SCORE be taken from the national organization and given to the Districts. The proposal was transmitted to higher SBA officials in the central office by Johnnie Albertson, then director of the Office of Program Delivery, but it never got off the ground.

SMALL BUSINESS DEVELOPMENT CENTERS -- This is an ongoing crisis and, in the words of James C. Sanders, former SBA Administrator, is the one over which both SCORE and SBDC have become paranoid.

Paranoia is the tendency towards excessive and/or irrational distrust of others, and it probably is in this context that Sanders spoke. While his analysis may be an accurate description of the current situation, it hardly explains the reasons for the paranoia if, in fact, paranoia actually does exist. A little background may shed some light on the subject.

Both SCORE and SBDC are SBA business development resources -- one a volunteer organization with long and deep ties with SBA; the other a relatively recent but wealthy and politically powerful network of offices affiliated with colleges and universities across the land and working for SBA under cooperative agreements. SCORE is sponsored by SBA and gets its funding through SBA's budget. SBDCs are funded directly by Congress and by matching grants from states. SCORE's manpower is unpaid; SBDCs' personnel are salaried.

Both groups are dedicated to helping small business, but their fields differ greatly in scope. SCORE is basically a counseling and a training resource. SBDCs were conceived as a sort of one-stop shopping centers for small business, places where small business studies and surveys are made, where small business needs are analyzed, and clearing houses where the efforts of federal, state and local groups, public and private, may be concentrated in the interests of small business.

SBDCs also sponsor and conduct workshops, and their salaried personnel do some one-on-one counseling. And therein lies the difficulty between SCORE and SBDC. The relationship tends to cast the two in the role of competitors on the one hand or as duplicators of service on the other.

It should be obvious that SBDC cannot take on full counseling service so effectively handled by SCORE without a tremendous increase in its payroll or by tapping the deep well of SCORE volunteers, something many fear might destroy SCORE's 25-year identity.

SBA's answer to all this has been to instruct SCORE and SBDC to cooperate with one another. This is an idealistic solution rather than a realistic one. It does not take the human element into account. There are as many interpretations of the word "cooperation" as there are people in SCORE, SBA and SBDC combined, some interpretations more selfish than others.

In some areas SCORE and SBDC seem to function cooperatively; in others they are not even speaking. And in a few areas cooperation has all but obliterated SCORE. When the two groups do cooperate on a case, arguments frequently erupt over which group gets credit. Credit is something more than mere jealousy -- although there may be some of that -- it is also an economic factor. While it may not be important to the client helped by the joint effort, credit is important to SCORE and SBDC since both need it to prove their effectiveness to SBA and to Congress.

Whether the conflict has degenerated into paranoia or not is moot. More important is the fact the crisis continues to interfere with the effective performance of SBA's mission.

PUBLICATIONS -- Here is an ongoing crisis that is just now getting a toe-hold in the SCORE organization.

Over a period of nearly 25 years SCORE has used millions of copies of SBA publications in one-on-one counseling, at workshops, in starter kits and for promotional purposes. They have been distributed under a policy set up in SBA's Standard Operating Procedures which says, "SCORE has continuous need for SBA publications useful to its work. Since SCORE assists SBA to fulfill its program, SBA publications are made available for SCORE program activities."

The catch is that the SOP does not say "free" publications, and when SBA decided to charge for its publications to recoup some of its expenses, SCORE was not excepted and now is faced with a tremendous cost item. Prices of the publications range from 50 cents to $1 each.

The problem is obvious. Except for the small income generated through workshops by some, but not all, chapters, SCORE's only source of income is from SBA. To pay for the SBA publications SBA now says SCORE must buy from SBA, SCORE must turn to SBA for the additional funds which, if that isn't passing the buck, is at least passing the buck back and forth.

There is a way to slap a bandage on the crisis -- the cost of publications distributed at workshops could be included in the fees charged for workshops -- but that does not solve the problem of paying for publications used by SCORE in ways other than in workshops. The bandage may reduce the size of the crisis but it won't make the crisis go away.

WHO'S IN CHARGE HERE, ANYWAY? -- This crisis is the shadowy type, lurking around the edges and making occasional but disruptive forays in the field. It becomes quite visible whenever local SBA officials insert themselves into the management of SCORE chapters.

The crisis began innocently enough when SBA formed its groups of counselors into chapters, thereby, in a small way, splitting chapter management. Through the ensuing years SBA has turned over to SCORE more of the management of its affairs, something that a few SCORE chapters and some SBA field officials have yet to learn.

It is said that SCORE chapters are autonomous. And they are. Up to a point. They are autonomous insofar as they operate within the guidelines of SCORE's Standard Operating Manual and SBA's Standard Operating Procedures, and both manuals place chapters under the management of the SCORE organization. Even so, some chapters and some SBA officials in the field still are of the opinion chapters are accountable only to SBA, not to SCORE.

The problem of "Who's in charge here?" has many tentacles, some of which reach into the national organization. Consider:

- SCORE cannot form a chapter without SBA's consent.
- SCORE members have to be approved by SBA.
- While District Representatives are appointed by Regional Representatives, appointments have to be approved by SBA. There are instances where SBA has appointed SCORE DRs without consulting with the RR.
- Volunteer directors at NSO must be approved by SBA.

- SCORE's Articles of Incorporation provide for the appointment of three members to the Board of Directors from outside of SCORE, but SBA has ruled that no appointments may be made without SBA's approval.

While SBA, through the years, has loosened its grip on the management of SCORE, it is apparent SBA has not yet gone the last mile, thereby perpetuating a dichotomy of leadership. SCORE seems to have a propensity for split entanglements. In its early years there was the SBA-ACTION relationship, followed by its own National SCORE Council-National SCORE Association combination. The self-govern versus governed crisis is hanging in there.

FUNDING -- Memorandum of Understanding. Cooperative Agreement. Grant. Travel Expenses. Clerical Support. Hidden Costs. Fees. Postage. Telephones. Office Space. Office Supplies. Printing. Advertising.

That is quite a lexicon of SCORE expenses.

Even though SCORE is a free service provided by volunteers, there is a dollar cost involved, a cost that in one way or another has to be paid if SCORE is to continue its service to small business.

SBA, to its chagrin, discovered that fact 25 years ago. It discovered that its new "free" service by volunteers was costing thousands of dollars in SBA staff time just to administer.

In the beginning, the volunteers were truly volunteers. If they made telephone calls, they paid for them out of their own pocket. If they wrote letters they used their own stationery and their own postage. If they visited clients they used their own cars and their own gasoline. And if, while visiting a client, someone stole their hubcaps, they paid for that, too. In other words, the volunteers had to pay for the privilege of being SCORE volunteers. Corrective action was needed.

Today a solution seems simple: Let SBA pick up the tab. Twenty-five years ago the solution was not that simple -- SBA had no congressional authority to pay expenses, although minor, to private persons even though those persons were providing a service to a government agency.

SBA, though, did come up with a solution; it permitted counselors to collect $5 from each client ($10 in some instances and even more if the travel involved was at great distance).

The solution was not a popular one. Many chapters never took advantage of it and individual members balked. They found it embarrassing to demand payment of $5 before they could start talking. Besides, many felt the matter of charging fees for their services cast a shadow on what was supposed to be a free program.

Not all members, of course, felt that way. Some saw fees as a way to augment their incomes.

Dr. Moon, in his thesis on the early days of SCORE, reports that one SCORE member went up and down the street, collecting $20 from every small business person who would talk to him.

Congress eventually empowered SBA to reimburse counselors for their out-of-pocket expenses, and that put an end to the unpopular and uncharacteristic fee program for counseling. The congressional action, though, increased SBA's cost for the program.

When SCORE was transferred to ACTION, ACTION was supposed to provide SCORE with travel expenses. This was a disaster. In the words of Orville Rummel, "ACTION was tight with the buck." At one point ACTION told SCORE that if it wanted any additional money, it would have to go to Congress for it or obtain it from former business affiliations.

When SCORE was transferred back to SBA, SCORE's travel budget under ACTION amounted to only $451,636, and a self-fulfilling prophecy came true. SCORE had to go to Congress and ask for an additional $1,117,000 to carry on its program.

Several attempts have been made to determine the true cost of the SCORE program, but the system contains so many variables Albert Einstein would need more than his theory of relativity to figure it out; much more is involved than the actual cash outlay, which was $2,500,000 for 1989. Other expenses which must be considered are such things as SBA staff time that is spent on SCORE, the value of office space in

SBA facilities or rented or donated space outside of SCORE offices, postage provided by SBA, use of the Federal Telecommunications System, office supplies, and now the cost of SBA publications.

The free SCORE program, manned by volunteers, carries a pretty heavy price tag. Does anyone want to make a guess? A clue: In 1975 SBA estimated the hidden costs in excess of $4,000,000.

And the costs keep rising. Every time SBA turns over to SCORE more of the management of the SCORE program, SBA may save some money but the cost to SCORE goes up. When SBA recently turned its Management Information System over to SCORE, the cost of handling the mechanics of the system had to be added to the budget of the National SCORE Office. Last year that amounted to $13,500.

The visible cost of SCORE -- the cash -- is provided by SBA each year under a Memorandum of Understanding. This money is divided into two parts -- travel expenses for counselors and funds for the National SCORE Office under a cooperative agreement. NSO's funds also are divided into two parts -- clerical support funds for the field and the amount needed for the operation of NSO.

Two other funds are involved in the SCORE program. One is the J. Howard Pew Freedom Trust fund that was made available to SCORE so it could open its national office. The grant of $40,000 was used as "seed" money to get the office open. Through interest and investments the fund now has grown somewhat and is used as a reserve for matters pertaining specifically to SCORE's nonprofit status.

The other fund really isn't a fund; it is made up of numerous chapter bank accounts, generated almost exclusively from workshop fees. The funds, almost all of them small, belong to the chapters and are used by them for such things as the purchase of office equipment, additional clerical support, small scholarships to worthy business school students, and now, the purchase of SBA publications.

Charging fees for workshops got off to a slow and rocky start. In the beginning, like SCORE counseling, workshops were free. It soon became apparent, though, that some things about workshops had price tags on them. Rental of adequate space is an example. Jay Lansford believes his chapter in Dallas was the first one to charge workshop fees. Dr. Pat LeMay Burr, then Associate Administrator for Management Assistance, gave guarded approval for chapters to charge workshop fees and recommended a range between $2 and $5. Even so, many chapters continued to provide free workshops.

On the other hand, those that did charge learned that fees had little or no effect on attendance and that the caliber of attendees improved. Fees eliminate "drop-ins," those people who come in off the street to get out of the cold in winter or the heat in summer. A cup of hot coffee or a soft drink provided additional incentives for the drop-ins.

Funding for SCORE -- the actual cash outlay -- always has been a problem. There seldom has been enough money to go around. For a period of time -- from FY81 through FY88 -- SCORE's cash funding remained static at just over $2.1 million. While he ascribed reasons for this, Lawrence R. Rosenbaum, now SBA Comptroller, stated in his 1984 review of the SCORE program that "SBA managers look upon SCORE members as second class citizens by reason of their lack of administrative support and financing." Professor Jeffrey L. Brudney of the Department of Political Science at the University of Georgia made a similar observation in an article published in 1986 in *Public Productivity Review.*

SBA has informally told SCORE that SBA has gone about as far as it can with direct funding, meanwhile raising the specter of user fees for counseling. This should have come as no surprise to SCORE: SBA, in the 1987 revision of its SOP for the Business Development program, used the words "user fees," "self support" and "cost recovery" nine times in the first four pages.

SCORE is as opposed today to user fees for counseling as it was 20 years ago. The Board of Directors of the SCORE Association has provided SBA with a resolution that emphatically states SCORE's stand.

Charles W. Heatherly is no longer with SBA, but he said recently that had he remained as the agency's acting Administrator he would have insisted that SCORE try user fees as an experiment to see if the concept would work.

"I found SCORE's stubbornness on the issue to be objectionable," he said. "On the national level it was a knee-jerk reaction."

With a view like that on one hand and SCORE's resistance on the other, user fees for counseling has the potential to become an emotional issue. Before that happens both sides might benefit from the views of Jay Lansford and Orville Rummel. In recent, independent interviews, both raised a pragmatic consideration.

The level of counseling skills among SCORE members ranges from poor to excellent, they said. Should clients, they ask, be required to pay for counseling that is unprofessional?

Rummel went a step further. "Since we do not know the level of counseling abilities of all our members," he said, "we might open ourselves to lawsuits if we charged fees for counseling."

There are those in SCORE who feel SCORE should go outside of SBA for financing. Joseph G. E. Knight, chairman of the SCORE Advisory Committee, is one. He feels the search for private funding from foundations has not been sufficiently explored and cites, as an example, the grant from the Pew Foundation.

And there are some who suggest that SCORE should become independent of SBA and work with it under a contract rather than a memorandum of understanding. They reckon, though, without consideration for the substantial hidden costs that have been part and parcel of the SCORE program for the past 25 years.

A single thread runs through these seven crises -- sufficient funding to operate SCORE efficiently. Since oracles have gone out of fashion, it is going to take all of Minerva's skill and wisdom to get SCORE off perennial short rations.

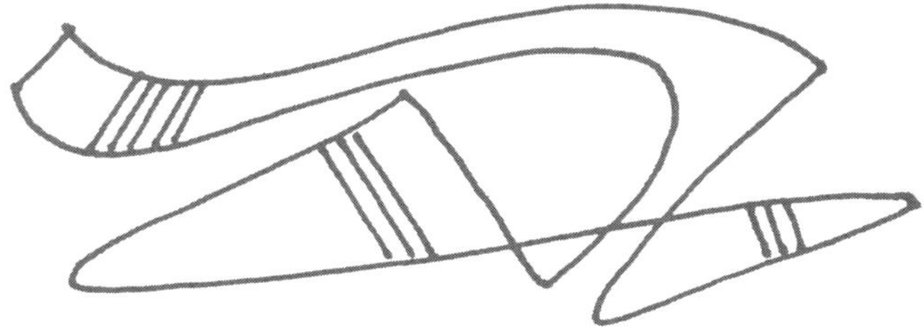

"The optimist proclaims that we live in the best of all possible worlds; the pessimist fears this is true."

Branch Cabell in The Silver Stallion

Chapter 9

Some Place, USA

(Mr. B goes to Washington.)

Lisa Benson had just started to prepare dinner when her husband came home. When he entered the kitchen from the garage he announced, "Break out the champagne! I've been elected Regional Representative! We're going to Washington!"

She gave him an owlish look. "Your strychnine is on the table. I've already had mine."

He kissed her and gave her an affectionate pat. "What's the matter with Washington?" he asked.

"I've been to Washington. I don't like it."

"Aw, come on. There's been a change of administrations since you were there."

"Let me think. Which Roosevelt was President when you took me there last, Mr. B? Was it Teddy or Franklin?"

She had called him "Mr. B" from the second day she had gone to work in the advertising department at his store. She had thought at first he was a stuffed shirt but soon had changed her mind. But the name had stuck through courtship, marriage, children and into retirement.

She squeezed his arm. "Seriously," she said, "I knew you'd be elected. I know you well enough to know that when you set your mind to something you usually get it done. But I admit I'm concerned. Are you sure you want to get yourself so involved? You've come home many times and said you were fed up, that you were going to quit SCORE and move to Tahiti. I've had our bags packed for a couple of years."

"Take them to Washington."

"Ha! I'd look fine going to a posh restaurant in a grass skirt and sandals."

His eyes twinkled. "Lisa, there are two things wrong with that statement. First, you look fine in anything. And second, we won't be going to any posh restaurants. Only my expenses will be paid by SCORE and on my government per diem the two of us will be eating at street corner kiosks. Why don't you pour us a glass of wine while I change my clothes?"

When Benson returned to the kitchen he was wearing a jogging suit.

"Why do you wear that thing?" Lisa demanded. "You don't jog."

"I know. But with all the emphasis on physical fitness I feel I have to make some concession to exercising. Besides, I subscribe to Orville Rummel's philosophy."

"What's that?"

"Keeping mentally active is more important than keeping physically active. I suspect a lot of people in SCORE feel the same way. That's one reason I ran for RR -- I like to reach for things that are too hard for me."

She raised her glass. "To Washington," she toasted. She took a sip of wine and made a wry face.

"Oh, come, Lisa. It's only for a few days every time we go."

"It wasn't Washington I was thinking about. I was doing some arithmetic."

"Arithmetic?"

She nodded. "If a person joins SCORE when he's 65, spends two or three years learning the ropes, two years as chapter chairman, another two years as DR and then a couple of terms as RR, he's going to be damned near 80 years old by the time he completes the circuit. What are you going to do when you get to be an octagenerian?"

He grinned. "Take you to Tahiti."

She cocked a disbelieving eyebrow at him and changed the subject. "You've got to start thinking about what you're going to do, now that you have become one of the anointed."

"Already have."

"I might have known. What do you plan to do?"

He apparently did not hear her. “There’s one thing that bothers me,” he told her. “Funding. As I look back over SCORE’s sometimes bumpy existence I get the impression that just about all of its problems can be lumped under one heading. Funding. It sometimes appears as though SBA is ambivalent about SCORE. On the one hand it wants and needs SCORE, while on the other hand it seems unwilling or unable to provide adequate funds to support it. I hope I’m wrong but if I’m not, the past -- as someone once observed -- will be the prologue to the future.”

"This is not the end. It is not even the beginning of the end. But it is, perhaps, the end of the beginning."

Winston Churchill, 1942

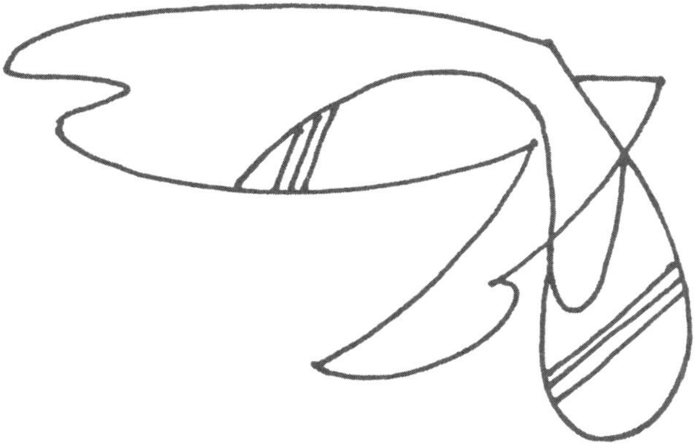

The National Leadership

SCORE's national organization has had several names. Started as the National Planning Committee in mid-1970, it became the National SCORE Committee at a meeting in Atlanta, Georgia, in October of that year. As work increased at the national level it became obvious that a stronger organization was needed, and in the process, the name of the organization was changed to the National SCORE Council in October 1973. Two years later, in August 1975, the Service Corps of Retired Executives was incorporated, and for eight years thereafter the SCORE program was administered in tandem by the Council and the Association. The Council was dissolved on December 31, 1982.

Regional Representatives, all of whom serve on the national Board of Directors, are elected for a two-year term and may serve two terms. Alternates are elected at the same time. Elections in odd-numbered Regions are held in odd-numbered years, while elections in even-numbered Regions are held in even-numbered years.

Following is a roster of the national Boards of Directors from calendar year 1970 to fiscal year 1990:

Calendar Year 1970[1]

Walter E. Gude, Region I
Robert B. Kyle, Region II
Julius Davidson, Region III
E. B. Wakefield, Region IV
Walter H. Channing, Region V, Chairman
Walter L. Kindle, Region VI
Don R. Zimmerman, Region VII
Irving M. Cohen, Region VIII
Henry M. Spack, Region IX
George W. Shields, Region X

Calendar Year 1971[2]

Walter E. Gude, Region I
Robert B. Kyle, Region II
Julius Davidson, Region III
E. B. Wakefield, Region IV*
Walter H. Channing, Region V, Chairman*
Walter L. Kindle, Region VI*
Don R. Zimmerman, Region VII
Forrest Atkinson, Region VIII
Henry M. Spack, Region IX
George W. Shields, Region X*

[1]Records in the National SCORE Office do not reflect the members of the Executive Committee for 1970, except for the Chairman.

[2]Members of the Executive Committee for 1971 are indicated by an asterisk.

Calendar Year 1972

Walter E. Gude, Region I
Hugo Galligan, Region II
Julius Davidson, Region III, Treasurer
Lee R. Maxwell, Region IV, Vice Chairman
Walter H. Channing, Region V, Chairman
Jay C. Lansford, Region VI
Don R. Zimmerman, Region VII
Donald L. Stewart, Region VIII
Henry M. Spack, Region IX, Secretary
Orville A. Rummel, Region X

Calendar Year 1973

Joseph G. E. Knight, Region I
William C. O'Brien, Region II
Walter P. O'Rourke, Region III
Lee R. Maxwell, Region IV, Chairman
Walter H. Channing, Region V[3]
Jay C. Lansford, Region VI, Vice Chairman
Don R. Zimmerman, Region VII
Donald L. Stewart, Region VIII
Arthur E. Kraus, Region IX, Treasurer
Orville A. Rummel, Region X, Secretary

Calendar Year 1974

Orville A. Rummel, Chairman
Joseph G. E. Knight, Region I, Secretary
William C. O'Brien, Region II
Walter P. O'Rourke, Region III
Lee R. Maxwell, Region IV
Walter H. Channing, Region V, Vice Chairman
Jay C. Lansford, Region VI, Treasurer

[3]Walter H. Channing was named Chairman Emeritus of the National SCORE Council.

Allen Burkhardt, Region VII
Lamburtus M. Stegeman, Region VIII
Arthur E. Kraus, Region IX
J. Rodger Mendenhall, Region X

Calendar Year 1975

Jay C. Lansford, Chairman
Joseph G. E. Knight, Region I, Secretary
William C. O'Brien, Region II, Treasurer
Walter P. O'Rourke, Region III
Lee R. Maxwell, Region IV
Walter H. Channing, Region V, Vice Chairman
Walter L. Kindle, Region VI
Allen Burkhardt, Region VII
Lamburtus M. Stegeman, Region VIII
Herbert J. L. Baum, Region IX
J. Rodger Mendenhall, Region X

Calendar Year 1976

Jay C. Lansford, Chairman
Joseph G. E. Knight, Region I, Secretary
Anthony A. Gigliotti, Region II
Walter P. O'Rourke, Region III
Herbert F. Barrett, Region IV
Walter H. Channing, Region V, Vice Chairman
William S. Miller, Region VI
Allen Burkhardt, Region VII
Lamburtus M. Stegeman, Region VIII
Herbert J. L. Baum, Region IX, Treasurer
Walter G. Garner, Region X

Calendar Year 1977

Joseph G. E. Knight, Chairman
Stanley A. Blanchard, Region I
Anthony A. Gigliotti, Region II
Walter P. O'Rourke, Region III

Barrett/Gilbert, Region IV[4]
Walter H. Channing, Region V, Vice Chairman
William S. Miller, Region VI, Secretary
Allen Burkhardt, Region VII
Lamburtus M. Stegeman, Region VIII
Herbert J. L. Baum, Region IX, Treasurer
Garner/Fields, Region X[5]

Calendar Year 1978

Joseph G. E. Knight, Chairman
Stanley A. Blanchard, Region I
Anthony A. Gigliotti, Region II
Walter P. O'Rourke, Region III
John S. Gilbert, Jr., Region IV
Walter H. Channing, Region V, Vice Chairman
Miller/Barnum, Region VI[6], Secretary
Arnold W. Koch, Region VII
Lewis E. Hollard, Region VIII
Herbert J. L. Baum, Region IX, Treasurer
Fields/Nieberg, Region X[7]

Calendar Year 1979

Herbert J. L. Baum, Chairman
Charles M. Dudley, Region I

[4]Herbert F. Barrett was representative through the October 1977 meeting and workshop in Albuquerque, New Mexico. John S. Gilbert, Jr. was listed as Region IV's representative at the NSC meeting held in Washington in November-December 1977, and no mention of Mr. Barrett was made in the minutes.

[5]Walter G. Garner was representing Region X at the beginning of 1977, but George Fields was listed as Region X's representative at the October 1977 meeting. There was no Region X representative at the November-December 1977 meeting.

[6]William S. Miller died December 9, 1978, and was replaced by his alternate, Lew Barnum.

[7]George Fields died September 1, 1978, and was replaced by his alternate, Carl H. Nieberg.

Anthony A. Gigliotti, Region II
Kerr/Bowman, Region III[8]
John S. Gilbert, Jr., Region IV, Secretary
Walter H. Channing, Region V, Vice Chairman
Lew Barnum, Region VI
Arnold W. Koch, Region VII, Treasurer
Lewis E. Hollard, Region VIII
James G. Black, Region IX
Carl H. Nieberg, Region X

Calendar Year 1980

Herbert J. L. Baum, Chairman
Charles M. Dudley, Region I
Paul K. Kiefer, Region II
Frederick C. Bowman, Jr., Region III
John S. Gilbert, Jr., Region IV, Secretary
Walter H. Channing, Region V, Vice Chairman
George A. Breffeilh, Region VI
Arnold W. Koch, Region VII, Treasurer
Helen Alexander, Region VIII
James G. Black, Region IX
Ted R. Stook, Region X

Calendar Year 1981

James G. Black, Chairman
Ted Rogers, Region I
Paul K. Kiefer, Region II
Jules A. Coelos, Jr., Region III
John S. Gilbert, Jr., Region IV, Secretary
Walter H. Channing, Region V
George A. Breffeilh, Region VI, Vice Chairman
Arnold W. Koch, Region VII, Treasurer
Helen Alexander, Region VIII
Ralph M. Hagen, Region IX
Ted R. Stook, Region X

[8]Donald C. Kerr resigned July 1, 1979, and was replaced by his alternate, Frederick C. Bowman, Jr.

Calendar Year 1982

James G. Black, Chairman
Ted Rogers, Region I, Treasurer
Kel Bamford, Region II
Jules A. Coelos, Jr., Region III
Richard D. Lee, Region IV
Walter H. Channing, Region V[9]
Melvin Lawson, Region VI
Alice J. Brown, Region VII
Helen Alexander, Region VIII, Vice Chairman
Ralph M. Hagen, Region IX, Secretary
Garfield R. Hubble, Region X

Calendar Year 1983

George A. Breffeilh, President
Ted Rogers, Region I
Kel Bamford, Region II, Vice President
Williams/Brillinger, Region III[10]
Richard D. Lee, Region IV
H. Torrey Walker, Region V
Melvin Lawson, Region VI, Secretary
Alice J. Brown, Region VII
Jack D. Berry, Region VIII[11]
James M. Stanley, Region IX
Garfield R. Hubble, Region X, Treasurer

Calendar Year 1984[12]

George A. Breffeilh, President
Ted Rogers, Region I, Treasurer
Kel Bamford, Region II, Vice President

[9]At the end of his term in 1982, Channing was elected President Emeritus, to serve on the Board for life.

[10]Robert E. Williams, Jr., died April 25, 1983, and was replaced by Charles J. Brillinger, his alternate.

[11]Helen Alexander resigned before the beginning of the year and was replaced by her alternate, Jack D. Berry.

[12]The calendar year 1984 ran from January 1 through September 30, 1984.

Charles J. Brillinger, Region III[13]
Richard D. Lee, Region IV
H. Torrey Walker, Region V, Secretary
John E. Foote, Region VI
Alice J. Brown, Region VII
Jack D. Berry, Region VIII
James M. Stanley, Region IX
John H. Titley, Region X

Fiscal Year 1985

Kel Bamford, President
Harry B. Matzen, Region I
Richard F. Brewster, Region II
Elliott/Smith/Dade, Region III[14]
Richard D. Lee, Region IV, Vice President
H. Torrey Walker, Region V, Secretary
John E. Foote, Region VI
King Herr, Region VII
Jack D. Berry, Region VIII
Paul Kirschner, Region IX
John H. Titley, Region X, Treasurer

Fiscal Year 1986

Kel Bamford, President
Harry B. Matzen, Region I
Robert C. Stockert, Region II
Willoughby S. Dade, Region III

[13]Between April 25 and May 22, 1984, Charles Brillinger resigned. His alternate, Charlie M. Smith, represented Region III at the May and September 1984 meetings.

[14]Joseph B. Elliott, Sr., was unable to perform his duties for health reasons and was represented by Charlie M. Smith, his alternate, until Mr. Smith's death on March 31, 1985. In April 1985 Mr. Elliott resigned and Willoughby S. Dade was appointed by the Association President to serve until an election could be held. In August 1985 Mr. Dade was declared the elected Representative for Region III.

A. B. Blankenship, Region IV
H. Torrey Walker, Region V, Vice President
John E. Foote, Region VI
King Herr, Region VII
Loehle Gast, Region VIII
Paul Kirschner, Region IX, Secretary
John H. Titley, Region X, Treasurer

Fiscal Year 1987

John H. Titley, President
Harry B. Matzen, Region I, Vice President
Robert C. Stockert, Region II, Secretary
Willoughby S. Dade, Region III
A. B. Blankenship, Region IV
Lester A. Stern, Region V
Foote/Kasper, Region VI[15]
King Herr, Region VII, Treasurer
Loehle Gast, Region VIII
Paul Kirschner, Region IX
Knight/Rader, Region X[16]

Fiscal Year 1988[17]

John H. Titley, President
Harry B. Matzen, Region I, Vice President
Robert C. Stockert, Region II, Secretary
Willoughby S. Dade, Region III
August A. Drufke, Region IV
Stern/Vorse, Region V[18]

[15]John E. Foote died January 9, 1987, and was replaced by his alternate, John F. Kasper.

[16]Clyde L. Knight died December 25, 1986, and was replaced by his alternate, Glen L. Rader.

[17]Kel Bamford, Past President, a non-voting member of the Board, resigned at the beginning of the fiscal year.

[18]Lester A. Stern died October 12, 1987, and was replaced by his alternate, John L. Vorse.

John F. Kasper, Region VI
King Herr, Region VII
Angle/Marshall, Region VIII[19]
Paul Kirschner, Region IX, Treasurer
Glen L. Rader, Region X

Fiscal Year 1989

Harry B. Matzen, President
Gordon B. Davis, Region I
Robert C. Stockert, Region II, Vice President
Robert W. Brown, Region III
August A. Drufke, Region IV
Robert C. Bertelsen, Region V
Kasper/Hummer, Region VI[20]
Edward F. Phillips, Region VII
Harold P. Marshall, Region VIII, Secretary
John Standish, Region IX
Glen L. Rader, Region X, Treasurer

Fiscal Year 1990

Harry B. Matzen, President
Gordon B. Davis, Region I
Curtis Locke, Region II
Robert W. Brown, Region III
Leo A. Perczak, Region IV
Robert C. Bertelsen, Region V, Vice President
Howard V. Hummer, Region VI
Edward F. Phillips, Region VII, Treasurer
James T. Garvey, Region VIII
John Standish, Region IX, Secretary
Howard O. Stone, Region X

[19]Christopher J. Angle resigned in October 1987 and was replaced by his alternate, Harold P. Marshall.

[20]John F. Kasper died April 12, 1989, and was replaced by his alternate, Howard V. Hummer.

SCORE's Ten Regions

(corresponding to SBA's Regions)

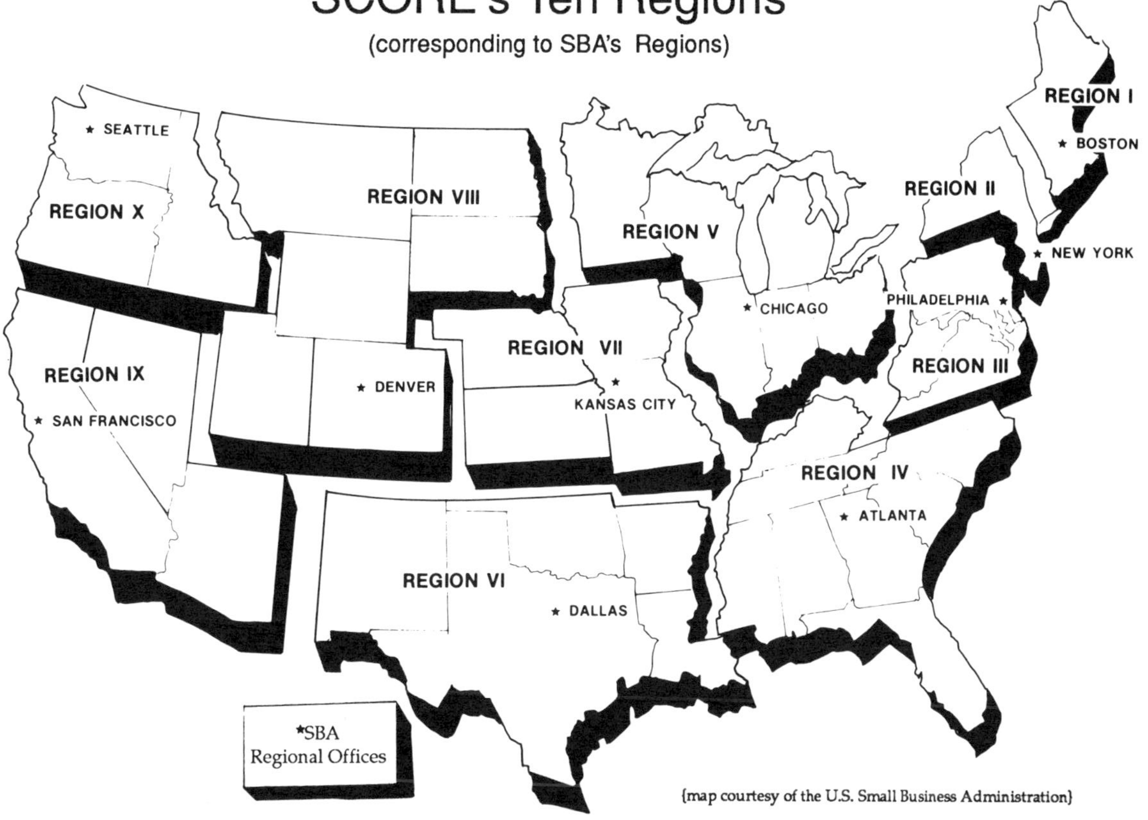

{map courtesy of the U.S. Small Business Administration}

A Tribute

What impels them to do it? What moves them to give up retirement, the comforts of their homes, the routines of their lives? What motivates them to strap on again a workaday harness for a position that pays no salary but demands a high degree of dedication and creativity?

The answers probably are as varied as the backgrounds of the 68 SCORE members who have filled director slots in the National SCORE Office in Washington, D. C., since the office was opened in March 1978. Contributing something of themselves for the betterment of SCORE has to be high on the list of reasons. Adventure, too, must play a part -- a chance to live and work in the commotion and excitement of the world's most prominent city.

In the beginning, volunteer directors were expected to serve only three months. The terms proved to be too short and were lengthened to six months and then to a year or more. For their efforts they have been provided with furnished apartments, travel expenses and monthly stipends to cover the cost of maintaining two homes. They also have had, almost at their fingertips, access to some of the most exciting and vibrant history the world has ever known.

So much for the directors. There is another side to the coin, a side that is seldom seen and one that too often has been taken for granted -- the role of spouses. They, too, have given up their homes and their routines to move to a strange city where friends and relatives are remote, trading comfort and security for an existence filled with time and little else.

As plans for the office were being formulated an obvious impediment was discovered -- travel expenses could be provided only for SCORE members. Spouses were not included. To get around that barrier, spouses had to become members of SCORE. That raised another problem. If they were members of SCORE and were being brought to Washington at SCORE's expense, there obviously had to be work for them to perform. So, in the early days of NSO, spouses periodically reported at the office to stuff envelopes and perform other routine chores, utilizing their hands but not their minds. The rules have since been changed; volunteer directors and their spouses now are brought to Washington by means of "relocation allowances."

Strangers from across the land, they met in Washington with only SCORE as a common denominator. That was sufficient. They banded together, established a camaraderie, and built friendships that have lasted far beyond the few short months together in the nation's capital. They shared trips to museums, galleries and monuments and, with their spouses, held cocktail parties, planned dinners at famous Washington area restaurants, and took weekend trips to nearby historic sites.

They not only survived what could have been a boring and lonely experience but, above all, they enriched the lives of their working spouses.

SCORE owes them much for the success of NSO.

Following is a list of the volunteer directors who have served at NSO, their positions, dates of service, and the Regions from which they came. Their spouses remain anonymous.

Executive Director

Jack H. Ducate (2/13/78 - 8/30/78) - VII
Claude W. Robinson (9/1/78 - 2/23/79) - VII
Robert W. Hurrle (2/26/79 - 7/20/79) - V
Phillip W. Wise (7/16/79 - 11/10/79) - X
William E. Gallagher (11/5/79 - 3/13/80) - VII
Stuart L. Forsyth (3/3/80 - 10/30/80) - X
Joseph T. Sylvester, Jr. (12/1/80 - 12/31/80) - VI
Arnold L. Lawson (1/5/81 - 6/27/81) - VIII
Ruth Jacobson (6/21/81 - 3/31/82) - VII
William J. Burke (4/1/82 - 10/15/82) - IV
Robert E. Copley (10/16/82 - 3/31/83) - VI
John H. M. Scribner (4/18/83 - 9/30/83) - IV
Paul F. Eiseman (10/1/83 - 6/30/84) - IX

[Executive Directorship became a paid position on July 1, 1984, and Eiseman continued in that position until his retirement in July 1987. The present Executive Director, John E. Daniels, has filled the position since July 6, 1987.]

Director of Membership and Training
(Recruitment and Training until 10/84)

Cecelia F. Stanton (3/6/78 - 10/31/78) - V
George Montooth (11/6/78 - 2/15/79) - IV
Edward A. Malling (2/15/79 - 6/1/79) - IV
Lester A. Stern (6/11/79 - 9/11/79) - V
Arnold L. Lawson (9/12/79 - 1/12/80) - VIII
Arnold L. Lawson (6/23/80 - 7/15/80) - VIII
George Montooth (7/16/80 - 2/2/81) - IV
Frank K. Kiple (2/28/81 - 8/29/81) - VII
Robert J. Lane (8/22/81 - 5/31/82) - IX
J. Albert Cairns (7/6/82 - 12/3/82) - IX
Paul F. Eiseman (1/4/83 - 7/24/83) - IX
Paul F. Eiseman (7/24/83 - 9/30/83, working from home) - IX
Kurt H. Felsenburg (10/1/84 - 4/1/86) - X
Frank J. Casabona (3/10/86 - 6/26/87) - II
Edward G. Welsh (6/29/87 - 5/31/88) - V
Gustav Berle (6/1/88 - 10/31/88) - IV
William W. Garry (11/1/88 - 10/31/89) - III

Director of Marketing (Public Relations and Publicity until 10/88)

Bryson Randolph (3/6/78 - 4/9/79) - III
Thomas E. Baynes (4/2/79 - 7/1/79) - IV
George V. Oliver (7/9/79 - 7/27/79) - IX
Irv Wasserman (9/4/79 - 2/14/80) - II
Elwyn A. Nellis (2/11/80 - 5/1/81) - X

Bertram R. Marks (4/26/81 - 6/14/81) - IV
Elwyn A. Nellis (6/14/81 - 9/5/81, working from home) - X
Leroy O. Wallin (9/6/81 - 3/15/82) - VIII
Leroy O. Wallin (3/16/82 - 12/31/82, working from home) - VIII
Robert J. Wade (1/4/83 - 7/8/83) - II
Charles H. Hall (7/11/83 - 1/31/84) - IV
Harry Riemen (2/1/84 - 7/24/84) - VI
Charles H. Hall (8/1/84 - 2/8/85) - IV
Elwyn A. Nellis (3/7/85 - 5/16/86) - X
Kenneth M. Abraham (5/1/86 - 4/25/87) - X
Gustav Berle (4/26/87 - 6/28/87, working from home) - IV
Gustav Berle (6/29/87 - 9/30/87) - IV
Cye Landy (10/1/87 - 6/30/88) - V
Gustav Berle (7/1/88 - 12/31/88) - IV
Paul Kirschner (12/1/88 - 11/30/89) - IX

Director of International Trade (Foreign Trade until 11/82) (position abolished 6/30/85 and reinstated 1/1/88)

Malvin J. Mayer (1/4/79 - 4/30/79) - I
John Bostick (5/13/79 - 9/20/79) - IV
John Weber (9/15/79 - 1/15/80) - IX
John M. Murphy (2/4/80 - 8/1/80) - VI
John Bostick (8/18/80 - 5/6/81) - IV
John H. M. Scribner (5/8/81 - 11/4/81) - IV
John H. M. Scribner (11/4/81 - 7/31/82, working from home) - IV
Paul D. Dale (8/1/82 - 11/15/82) - VII
Paul D. Dale (11/16/82 - 1/31/83, working from home) - VII
William D. Schenk (1/1/83 - 7/31/83) - IV
Arthur D. Shaver (8/1/83 - 1/31/84) - VII
Paul M. White, Jr. (1/1/84 - 7/25/84) - IV
Clifford H. Lane (8/1/84 - 6/30/85) - III

Robert A. Slenes (1/1/88 - 12/31/88) - IX
David C. Buffam (1/1/89 - 12/31/89) - X

Director of Energy Conservation (position abolished 7/81)

C. Alfred de Vyver (10/30/78 - 4/27/79) - I
Maurice C. Swanson (4/23/79 - 8/1/79) - II
James L. Ingoldsby (8/9/79 - 12/6/79) - IX
C. Alfred de Vyver (3/3/80 - 5/1/80) - I
Barnett French (6/18/80 - 6/30/81, working from home) - VI

Director of Crime Loss Prevention (position abolished 7/81)

Joseph T. Sylvester, Jr. (8/13/79 - 12/31/80, working from home) - VI
Jack D. Penland (1/1/81 - 6/30/81, working from home) - VI

Other SCORE Volunteers Serving at the National SCORE Office

Julius Davidson, Budget and Finance Director (3/1/78 - 12/31/81) - III
Walter P. O'Rourke, General Counsel (3/1/78 - 2/1/82) - III
Arthur J. Gang, General Counsel (6/10/82 - 11/30/85); Counsel to the President (1/1/86 - present) - III
Jules A. Coelos, Jr., Budget and Finance Director (1/1/83 - 9/30/84, working from home) - III
Alfred Meisner, Associate General Counsel (9/7/83 - 11/30/85); General Counsel (12/1/85 - present) - III
Alice J. Brown, Women's Business Ownership Director (1/1/84 - present, working from home) - VII

Ted Rogers, Budget and Finance Director (10/1/84 - present, working from home) - I

Elwyn A. Nellis, Editor of The SAVANT (5/16/86 - 4/30/88, working from home) - X

Allen J. Farrar, Associate General Counsel (8/6/86 - present) - III

John B. Flanagan, Special Projects Director (9/29/87 - 6/30/88) - III

Martin F. Saper, Veterans Affairs Director (1/1/88 - present, working from home) - IV

King Herr, Rural Development Director (6/1/88 - present, working from home) - VII

Glen L. Rader, Youth Entrepreneurship Director (6/1/88 - present, working from home) - X

Wallace E. Velander, ADP Director (6/1/88 - present) - III

Jewel F. Lewis, Associate General Counsel (1/11/89 - present) - III

Bibliography

Brudney, Jeffrey L., "The SBA and SCORE: Coproducing Management Assistance Services," *Public Productivity Review*, no. 40 (1986)

Dutton, William S., "They Retired -- and Got Busy," *Saturday Evening Post*, June 16, 1951

Moon, Grant C., "An Evaluation of Selected Management Aspects of the SBA SCORE Program," copyright 1968; original title: "Selected Sociological, Economic and Political Values and Implications of the Management Counseling Program for Small Business Owners and Managers Entitled SCORE (Service Corps of Retired Executives)," unpublished Ph.D. dissertation, George Washington University, 1966

National SCORE Office files

Personal files of:

Herbert J. L. Baum
Walter H. Channing
Joseph G. E. Knight
Orville A. Rummel

Personal interviews with:

Johnnie L. Albertson on October 10, 1988
Herbert J. L. Baum on November 18, 1988

James G. Black on November 17, 1988
Pat LeMay Burr on October 3, 1988
Walter H. Channing on November 7, 1988
Patricia M. Cloherty on November 9, 1988
Charles W. Heatherly on October 20, 1988
Joseph G. E. Knight on November 8, 1988
Jay C. Lansford on November 15, 1988
Richard D. Lee on November 12, 1988
Orville A. Rummel on November 21, 1988
James C. Sanders on October 18, 1988
Lincoln A. Simon on November 23, 1988

Parris, Addison W., *The Small Business Administration.* New York: Frederick A. Praeger, 1968

Rankin, Allen, "Retirement? It's the Time of His Life!", *Reader's Digest*, January 1963

Rockville Consulting Group, Major Impact Study of SBA Management Assistance Programs (Washington, D. C.: U. S. SBA, 1980)

Rosenbaum, Lawrence R., *Review of the Service Corps of Retired Executives Program* (Washington, D. C.: U. S. Small Business Administration, 1984)

Study of the Organization of the Service Corps of Retired Executives, with Recommendations for Changes, prepared by a special task force appointed by the Service Corps of Retired Executives upon the recommendation of the U. S. Small Business Administration, Washington, D. C., 1983

Tupper, Harmon, "SCORE Spells Help for the Small Businessman," *Reader's Digest*, March 1967

Index